PRAYER – THE HEART OF THE GOSPELS

In gratitude for
the friendship, support and inspiration of my
Sisters and Brothers in Carmel

Faithful friends are beyond price;
there is no measuring their worth.
(Ecclesiasticus 6:15)

James McCaffrey OCD

Prayer
– The Heart of the Gospels

the columba press

First published in 2008 by
the columba press
55A Spruce Avenue, Stillorgan Industrial Park,
Blackrock, Co Dublin

Cover by Bill Bolger
Origination by The Columba Press
Printed in Ireland by ColourBooks Ltd, Dublin

ISBN 1 85607 612 8

Acknowledgements
Biblical quotations are from the New Revised Standard Version, copy-
right © 1989, by the Division of Christian Education of the National
Council of the Churches of Christ in the USA, and are used by permission. All rights reserved. Quotations from the psalms are from the Grail
version in *The Psalms: A New Translation*, London: Fontana, 1963.

Table of Contents

Preface

Praying, reading and teaching the scriptures over many years, I have discovered their supreme importance for a better and deeper understanding of the spiritual life. It is this experience that has urged me to write this book and explore the biblical foundations of the mystery of Christian prayer. What I have written here is meant as a help to discover or rediscover the riches of the gospels. In no way is it meant as a substitute for them. We can all read about prayer in a book. But what really matters is actually to pray. For this reason, the book is not intended as mere theory, nor is it a purely academic study of prayer in the gospels. Rather, it is my hope that this book will inspire the reader to persevere faithfully in the search for an ever-deeper life of communion with God, praying – and living – in the spirit of the gospels after the example of Jesus. The whole purpose of what I have written is to help others – and myself – actually to pray.

As an aid to praying the word of God and relating it to our lives, the book begins with a Prologue which provides an outline of the practice of *lectio divina* – the ancient monastic way of praying with scripture but presented here in a form accessible to all. As well as explaining each of the traditional stages, this outline also includes a section on how to practise *lectio* in a group. This initial explanation takes on concrete form in a guided *lectio divina* at the end of each chapter: here, a gospel passage is given, followed by indications of how each of the stages might develop in praying this sacred text. In addition, an appendix at the end of the book provides the prayer texts from each gospel.

Also concluding each chapter is a short selection of *questions for reflection*. These are based on the content of the chapter concerned and focus on both prayer and the central insight into Jesus of the gospel in question. These suggestions may also be helpful for Bible study groups, as well as for reflection within the context of a prayer group or simply for use by individuals. The two exercises – study and *lectio divina* – should not, however, be seen as unrelated activities: study of the gospels cannot fail to feed into prayer, while prayerful reflection lends to knowledge an added dimension and depth. As Vatican II reminds us: 'Prayer should accompany the reading of sacred scripture' (*DV* 25).[1]

We now come to the main chapters of the book. The first four introduce the reader to the lessons on prayer in each of the gospels in turn. The treatment of this theme is inspired by the teaching of Vatican II in its *Dogmatic Constitution on Divine Revelation* (*DV* 19). This document reveals both the development of the gospel tradition, and also the uniqueness of each evangelist in drawing on the tradition. These twin aspects illuminate – and are illuminated by – the mystery of prayer in the gospels.

This statement of the Council for a better understanding of the origin of the gospels (*DV* 19) speaks of three stages: what Jesus did and taught during his earthly ministry; the tradition (oral and written), handed on in the early Christian community, enlightened by the Spirit; and the written texts of the gospels. The document therefore provides an ideal perspective from which to explore the teachings on prayer special to each of the evangelists, in the context of a developing tradition. Mark, for example, is generally accepted as the earliest of the four; so perhaps it is not surprising that his gospel contains fewer of the sayings of Jesus on prayer.

The Our Father is a helpful and representative example in that it is indicative of the general development in gospel prayer teaching. Early intimations of it in Mark (Mk 11:25; 14:38) are expanded and developed in Matthew (Mt 6:9-15) and Luke (Lk 11:2-4), and reappear there within the framework of two distinct

---

1. *DV = Dei Verbum (Dogmatic Constitution on Divine Revelation)*.

forms of the prayer. Even within the Our Father itself, we find a development: Matthew expands on Luke with the additional petition, 'Your will be done' (Mt 6:10). Finally, the high point comes in John, the last of the gospels. Here, we find unmistakable echoes of the Our Father – 'I have come ... not to do my own will, but the will of him who sent me ... protect them from the evil one' (Jn 6:38; 17:15; cf Mt 6:13) – and in the priestly prayer Jesus speaks to his, and our, Father in union with his disciples (Jn 17; cf Mt 6:9; Lk 11:2), taking all believers with him into the heart of the mystery of God. As we explore in this way the expanding prayer tradition of the gospels, we can see how the early church, right from the outset, penetrated ever more deeply, under the action of the Spirit, into the mystery of Jesus at prayer.

The *Dogmatic Constitution on Divine Revelation* also tells us that the evangelists 'selected', 'synthesised' and 'explicated' what they found as a living tradition in the early Christian community (*DV* 19). They did this in the light of their own central insight into Jesus, which serves to unify each individual gospel. Each one highlights a facet of the inexhaustible mystery of God revealed in Jesus. And this central insight is intimately linked with the evangelists' understanding of prayer.

The Jesus of Mark is the Suffering Servant of Isaiah (cf Is 52:13–53:12) – rejected, despised, and misunderstood even by his own. This is reflected in the starkness of Mark's style and in his treatment of prayer. He brings out contrasts and underscores the paradox: the cross is the scandal that reveals Jesus as the Son of God. And the triumph of Jesus emerges from his apparent failure and desolation, expressed in his prayer on the cross: 'My God, my God, why have you forsaken me?' (Mk 15:34). Finally, his death results in an act of faith by a pagan centurion of Rome's imperial army: 'Truly this man was God's Son!' (Mk 15:39). For Mark, prayer is a journey of faith out of darkness and into the light (cf Mk 4:26-29). His gospel is one of veiled epiphanies.

In Matthew, Jesus is the obedient Israelite, an insight again reflected in the evangelist's style and in his special understanding of prayer. His writing is smooth and polished by comparison with Mark's somewhat uneven narrative; and Matthew's didactic and extended discourses are repeatedly enriched with Old Testament echoes, implicit and explicit, to reinforce the lesson that Jesus is the definitive fulfilment of God's will in a new covenant (cf Mt 5:17-18). He does not hesitate to tell us, in the words of Jesus, that the ideal disciple is 'whoever does the will of my Father in heaven' (Mt 12:50). So, he presents prayer as essentially an act of surrender to God's will after the model of Jesus. This is exemplified in the petition he adds to the Our Father: 'Your will be done' (Mt 6:10).

Luke's Jesus is the Spirit-filled prophet who proclaims the word, to which he has first listened in silence. This, too, is mirrored in the style and teaching of the gospel. As a writer of salvation history which he continues in Acts, Luke in his gospel describes the events in a well-ordered sequence. Notably, at the turning-points in the unfolding of God's plan, he presents Jesus to us in quiet prayer. For Luke, to pray is essentially to listen. This is embodied in Mary of Bethany who sat at the feet of Jesus and listened to his word (Lk 10:38-42).

In the fourth gospel, Jesus is the manifestation of God in person. This, in turn, is reflected in the style and teaching of John, and especially in the priestly prayer (Jn 17) which is like a replica in miniature of his whole gospel. Using a vocabulary of revelation, this prayer expresses the intimate union between Father, Son and believers, which is essentially what it means to pray 'in the name', so characteristic of the fourth gospel: 'I will do whatever you ask in my name ... I have made your name known' (Jn 14:13; 17:6).

Finally, it would not be possible to have a full understanding of prayer in the gospels without also exploring the role of the Holy Spirit. The Spirit is fundamental to any understanding of the word of God and the mystery of prayer, as well as to the practice of prayer itself. So chapter 5, 'Praying with the Holy Spirit', provides insights into the profound riches of the mysterious promptings of the Spirit in prayer. This is shown within the general framework of John's gospel, with special emphasis given to his incomparable Paraclete passages.

Just as the Prologue takes Mary as the exemplar for the various aspects of *lectio divina*, so the Epilogue provides a portrait of Mary as the inspiration for every disciple who wishes to pray in the spirit of the gospels. The mystery of the Mother of Jesus, like the mystery of prayer itself, developed only gradually in the gospel tradition. There is little in Mark to suggest the deeper understanding of her role in the later gospels of Matthew, Luke and John. Her place in God's plan of redemption is part of the church's inner secret and unfolds progressively through the workings of the Spirit in the early community of believers. Furthermore, Mary is a perfect model of communion with God, in harmony with the way each evangelist presents to us the mystery of prayer. Praying with the scriptures, however, must ultimately pass into actual life experience, as it did in Mary's own life, and bear fruit in the loving service of others. This, the acid test of all authentic Christian prayer, is again what it means to share in the mystery of Christ's own prayer – its depths and its fruitfulness.

I would like to end with a brief word of thanks to all who have helped me by their encouragement and careful reading of this book, either in whole or in part, with special mention of Dr Joanne Mosley, my colleague as assistant editor of our Carmelite magazine *Mount Carmel*. I would also like to express my gratitude to Mgr Joseph Reilly of Seton Hall University NJ who, as Director of the International Institute for Clergy Formation, invited me to share the contents of this book with so many of my fellow priests. Their interest and comments have confirmed for me the universal value and appeal of a prayerful reading of the gospels and strengthened me in my calling, as a Carmelite, to a life of prayer.

How to Read and Pray the Gospels

The importance of lectio divina
In recent times, *lectio divina*, a traditional approach to a personal and collective praying of the scriptures, has taken on renewed emphasis. As Pope Benedict XVI said at the Chrism Mass on Holy Thursday, 2006: 'Listening to [Jesus] – in *lectio divina*, that is, reading sacred scripture in a non-academic but spiritual way … we learn to encounter Jesus present, who speaks to us. We must reason and reflect, before him and with him, on his words and actions. The reading of sacred scripture is prayer, it must be prayer – it must emerge from prayer and lead to prayer.'

Here, the pope is echoing the call of Vatican II exhorting us to reflect often and prayerfully on the word of God, in order 'to learn by frequent reading of the divine scriptures the "excelling knowledge of Jesus Christ" (Phil 3:8)' (*DV* 25). We recall the celebrated saying of Jerome: 'Ignorance of the scriptures is ignorance of Christ.'[1] Moreover, the council also reminds us that the gospels must always take pride of place: 'It is common knowledge that among all the scriptures, even those of the New Testament, the gospels have a special pre-eminence, and rightly so, for they are the principal witness of the life and teaching of the incarnate Word, our Saviour' (*DV* 18). Four of the five chapters in this book are directly concerned with the example of the praying Jesus in the gospels and with his teachings on prayer.

With the mind and heart of Mary
The insights of the gospels on prayer, however beautiful and sublime, can so easily remain at the level of theory. They need to be translated into an actual experience of praying with scripture.

---

1. *Commentary on Isaiah*, Prol.: PL 24, 17, quoted in *DV* 25.

To read the sacred word in the spirit of the gospels is to pray it with the mind and heart of Mary – *the* gospel woman of prayer. It is to put on the inner dispositions of her intimate relationship with her Son, in complete openness to the action of the Spirit. She is a living witness to the quiet workings of God's grace within her as she responds in concrete circumstances to God's word. A glance at her life provides us with some practical helps that we all need, as individuals and as groups, for a simple and renewed approach to the traditional *lectio divina* in a way that is accessible to all.

Certain dispositions are required for the word to take root in us. Mary provides a model for all of them. She is, before anything, a woman who listens in awe and reverence to the word of God.[2] There are no barriers when Mary listens; there must be none for us either. She is at ease, relaxed with God, when the angel reassures her, 'Do not be afraid' (Lk 1:30). Mary is aware that she is the object of God's special love. This awareness of his love for us must also be our entry point into prayer: we, too, 'have found favour with God' (Lk 1:30). Mary stands before God just as she is – 'the servant of the Lord' (Lk 1:38) – and he looks 'with favour on the lowliness of his servant' (Lk 1:48). We, too, come before God without pretence, pose or façade: weak, frail, vulnerable and contrite sinners, unmasked in our emptiness and need before a God whose 'mercy is … from generation to generation' (Lk 1:50). That great teacher of prayer, Teresa of Avila, recommends that we should begin our prayer with an act of contrition, the *Confiteor* (WP 26:1).[3] Mary knows that he who is mighty has done – and can still do – great things for her. We should start with the same attitude of trust, ready to risk everything on the truth of God's word. We can say all this, if we wish,

---

2. As Vatican II exhorts us: 'Christians should receive [the scriptures] with reverence' (*DV* 15).

3. References to the works of Teresa of Avila are taken from *The Collected Works of St Teresa of Avila*, 3 vols, Washington, DC: ICS Publications, 1987, 1980 & 1985. Works quoted are: *L = The Book of Her Life*; *WP = The Way of Perfection*; *IC = The Interior Castle*; *F = The Book of Her Foundations*.

in an eloquently simple gesture with empty and upturned hands, waiting to receive whatever God wants to say to us and ask of us in prayer.

Mary's faith unlocks the secret of her approach to the word: 'Blessed is she who believed that there would be a fulfilment of what was spoken to her by the Lord' (Lk 1:45). We, too, come to the gospels in a spirit of faith – a questioning faith like hers, ever-searching for a deeper meaning and understanding of the mystery of her Son and its bearing, here and now, on our lives. So, we begin with an act of faith, opening our inner eye to the ac-tion of the Spirit who will 'come upon' us as he did for Mary (Lk 1:35). We invoke the Holy Spirit. For this, we may choose a prayer of our own liking. Perhaps it will be a traditional one such as: 'Come, Holy Spirit!' Or, if we prefer, we can formulate a prayer in our own words. Reading the gospels, open with Mary to the action of the Spirit, will centre us directly on her Son. We must always bear in mind that the inspired texts, both the old and the new, speak of him: 'The New Testament is hidden in the Old and the Old is made manifest in the New.'[4] So, we focus on Jesus – like Mary, who was the first to fix her eyes on the Word made flesh. To contemplate with the heart of Mary is to have eyes for Jesus – Jesus alone (cf Mk 9:8).

A helpful method

There are many ways of practising *lectio divina*, and it can be done either individually or within a group.[5] Traditionally, it is divided into four stages: reading (*lectio*), meditation (*meditatio*), prayer (*oratio*) and contemplation (*contemplatio*). A fifth is some-times added: action (*actio*). They provide a broad and helpful outline for many, covering the whole ascending movement of

---

4. Augustine, *Quest. In Hept.*, 2, 73: PL 34, 623.
5. See the publications listed in James McCaffrey OCD, *The Carmelite Charism: Exploring the Biblical Roots*, Dublin: Veritas, 2004, p 36, note 24; see also: Mario Masini, *Lectio Divina: An Ancient Prayer that is Ever New*, New York: Alba House, 1998; M Basil Pennington OCSO, *Lectio Divina: Renewing the Ancient Practice of Praying the Scriptures*, New York: Crossroad, 1998.

prayer. But they are not meant as a straitjacket, something rigid and inflexible. Like the seven mansions that mark the progressive journey in prayer in Teresa of Avila's *Interior Castle*, these stages are not mutually exclusive. In fact, they are intimately connected, complementing each other beautifully: we can be praying while we read, and contemplating while we ponder.

Reading:

We read the word calmly. We must try to still the mind and compose the senses as best we can, for example by breathing slowly, deeply and rhythmically. A relaxation technique can be helpful for some to create an inner attitude or disposition of contemplative calm as a prelude to reading the word.[6] We must also read the word with reverence, accepting it 'not as a human word but as what it really is, God's word' (1 Thess 2:13). Vatican II reminds us: 'We hear [God] when we read the divine sayings.'[7] Selecting a short passage, we repeat it slowly, more than once, articulating each word and phrase attentively and distinctly, aloud if we prefer. We may repeat the reading as often as time permits, lingering on the word and rediscovering each time its perennial freshness and newness, as Mary did. This kind of reading calls for a calm, quiet rhythm and an unhurried, lingering pace, helping us to become familiar with the word of God, etching it firmly in the memory and opening our minds to assimilate the mysteries of the Lord's life concealed in his word. In this way, the unfathomable riches of these mysteries will be able to unfold gradually.[8] We wait patiently for a word or phrase to stand out from the page for us. We do not go in search of it; we let it come, unbidden.

---

6. For publications on relaxation techniques in the context of prayer, see James McCaffrey, *The Carmelite Charism, op. cit.*, p 36, note 23.
7. *DV* 25, quoting St Ambrose, *On the Duties of Ministers*, I, 20, 88: PL 16, 50.
8. Few have expressed these inexhaustible riches more beautifully than St Ephraem: see *Divine Office*, vol I, pp 518-9.

Meditation:

We reflect on the word, 'living and active, sharper than any two-edged sword, piercing until it divides soul from spirit' (Heb 4:12). Savouring the word or phrase which comes to us spontaneously from our reading, we now mull over it with the mind. Like Mary, we meditate on the word, 'treasuring' and 'pondering' it in our hearts (cf Lk 2:19), discerning the hidden depths of each phrase. We may also let the word be enriched by biblical associations that come to us, clinging to it and opening up further the depths of the mystery concealed and revealed in God's word. Meditation is not an academic exercise or a study. It is an openness to the Spirit, letting the word move from the head to the heart. This is often a painful journey into the very centre of our being. We read the word with our life's experience and let our life's experience be read by it in turn. Gradually, we ourselves become a living word. This has nothing to do with sublime heights beyond our reach: it is the effect of direct contact with the power of God's saving love, released and enkindled within us through the word by the Spirit.

Prayer:

We now begin to pray the word 'out of the abundance of the heart' (Mt 12:34). It is only love that can change and transform us. The word touches and enflames us and we let our hearts go out in love. We lay bare before the Lord whatever surfaces spontaneously from deep within us as we ponder the word. Like Mary, we may find ourselves brimming with thanksgiving and praise: 'The Mighty One has done great things for me, and holy is his name' (Lk 1:49). Or we might just give ourselves over to an inner current of joy: 'My spirit rejoices in God my Saviour' (Lk 1:47). We may feel at times bewildered and confused as Mary did: 'How can this be? ... [She] did not understand what he said to them' (Lk 1:34; 2:50), while we wrestle perhaps with an urgent problem, seeking an answer that never seems to come: 'Why have you treated us like this?' (Lk 2:48). We voice in silence all our inmost thoughts and desires, letting the aspirations pour out with a fling of the heart to the heart of the God who first loved us (cf 1 Jn 4:10). The essential is to enter into direct communion with God, person-to-person, in a dialogue of love, arising from wellsprings in the deep heart's core. Teresa of Avila says that prayer does not consist in thinking much but in loving much (*F* 5:2; cf *IC* IV:1:7).

Contemplation:

We now begin to contemplate the word in silence with a simple glance of love towards Jesus, whom faith reveals as present in his word, so 'that [we] may be strengthened in [our] inner being with power through his Spirit, and that Christ may dwell in [our] hearts through faith, as [we] are being rooted and grounded in love' (Eph 3:16-17). Teresa of Avila advises: 'One should just remain there in his presence with the intellect quiet … occupy ourselves in looking at Christ who is looking at us' (*L* 13:22). We are drawn quietly into the deep mystery of his person which the word conceals and reveals. The phrase 'Be still and know' (Ps 45:11) takes on ever-deeper and unexpected depths. We let everything fade into a calm, peaceful and quiet experience of God's presence in his word. Stay in the silence, rest in it, listen to it. Wordless, we stand in spirit with Mary, as she once 'gazed in sheer wonder' on her Son lying in a manger (*R* 9)[9] and later stood quietly at the foot of the cross, communing with him in silent love and accepting from him her future mission. Ultimately, to contemplate the word is to be conformed to the likeness of Mary's Son: 'all of us, with unveiled faces, seeing the glory of the Lord as though reflected in a mirror, are being transformed into the same image from one degree of glory to another; for this comes from the Lord, the Spirit' (2 Cor 3:18).

---

9. References to the works of John of the Cross are taken from *The Collected Works of Saint John of the Cross*, Washington, DC: ICS Publications, 1991. Works quoted are: *A = The Ascent of Mount Carmel*; *LF = The Living Flame of Love*; *P = Poems*; *R = Romances*.

Action:

We now begin to translate the word into action, mindful to be 'doers of the word, and not merely hearers who deceive themselves' (Jas 1:22). It is not sufficient merely to accept the word in theory, we must respond to it in practice with a firm resolution as Mary did: 'Let it be to me according to your word' (Lk 1:38; *RSV*). We know that 'the word of God is living and active … at work in [us] believers' (Heb 4:12; 1 Thess 2:13), bearing fruit in service: 'You will know them by their fruits' (Mt 7:16). Teresa of Avila reminds us: 'This is the reason for prayer … the birth always of good works, good works' (*IC* VII:4:6). These works take many forms. Here, too, Mary's example points the way: her compassion, responding to a neighbour in need, just as she 'set out and went with haste to a Judean town in the hill country' (Lk 1:39) to tend to her cousin Elizabeth; her witness, inviting others to come and listen to Jesus: 'Do whatever he tells you' (Jn 2:5), and announcing to the world the wonders of God's goodness: 'My soul magnifies the Lord' (Lk 1:46); her solidarity with the community of believers as Mary was joined in continuous prayer with the first disciples (cf Acts 1:14), praying for them and with them. We, too, are intimately linked with Mary, mother of God and mother of the church: we are always one, like her, with the whole community of believers when we pray – sisters and brothers in the same great family of the church.

Sharing:

This is not a sixth stage of *lectio divina* but denotes what has traditionally been called *collatio* (literally: 'bringing together'), when we pray the word in a group.[10] It is an ecclesial experience: 'For where two or three are gathered in my name, I am there among them' (Mt 18:20). We draw strength from the shared experience of a prayerful reading of the gospels, and we communicate to others in the group the fruits of our prayer. This we do in whatever way the Spirit directs us to make Christ present to

---

10. For a treatment and suggested methods of group *lectio*, see Pennington, *op. cit.*, pp 123-33.

them, through the power of the word we have heard, pondered, and contemplated in prayer. The psalmist, we recall, felt urged to speak the word in the community of believers: 'My lips I have not sealed ... I have not hidden your love and your truth from the great assembly' (Ps 39:10-11). *Lectio* – through the power of the word – is prayer in union with all believers, whether practised individually or in a group. It enriches the whole community.[11]

After invoking the Holy Spirit, we begin our group *lectio divina* by reading the word aloud, slowly, and pausing between phrases, to allow the word to sink into the depths of our hearts. After the reading or readings, the individual members of the group may be invited to speak aloud the word or phrase that stands out for them – though without giving any commentary – to let that word have its effect on others. There is then a short period of meditation, in which we ponder the mystery of God contained in the word and the impact it may have on our lives. If the group would like to share these insights, they should feel free to do so, but always to enrich and enlighten rather than to preach; this should be done in an appropriate way, without pouring out personal confidences that would be more fittingly exposed in one-to-one spiritual direction or in the sacrament of reconciliation. Our period of prayer, which follows, will consist of spontaneous offerings of silent praise, thanksgiving, repentance and petition. Finally, this will merge into an ever-deeper stillness of contemplation, gazing on God and opening ourselves to the challenge of the word in our daily lives. Each group, however, should feel perfectly at ease in the way it chooses to follow the stages. For a living exchange with God, there is no fixed set of rules except one: 'Where the Spirit of the Lord is, there is freedom' (2 Cor 3:17).

'Never lose heart'
We might add, by way of postscript, the need for perseverance in *lectio divina*. The phrase 'determined determination', or 'res-

---

11. See Carlos Mesters O Carm, *Lectio Divina*, Melbourne: Carmelite Communications, 1999, p 59.

olute determination', runs like a refrain through the teaching of Teresa of Avila on prayer (*WP* 21:2). *Lectio divina* is not designed merely as a one-off experience in our lives: it provides a concrete and flexible pattern of prayer for use by anyone at any time. There will be moments of dryness, a desert experience. The page before us will not always 'speak' to us immediately. It may be that the seed of the word is still sinking into the soil of our hearts. It will thrust up shoots at its proper time. In the words of Thérèse of Lisieux: 'Frequently, we descend into the fertile valleys where our heart loves to nourish itself, the *vast field of the scriptures* which has so many times opened before us to pour out its rich treasures in our favour; this *vast field* seems to us to be a desert, arid and without water … We *know no longer* where *we are*; instead of peace and light, we find only turmoil or at least darkness … We do not know … but Jesus really knows. He sees our sadness and suddenly his gentle voice makes itself heard, a voice more gentle than the springtime breeze.'[12]

As we can see, reading and praying the word may be a slow, gradual, imperceptible process. The spiritual life is, in any case, a marathon, not a sprint: we must walk at God's pace, as Mary did when puzzling over the angel's enigmatic message and awaiting its unfolding in God's own time. It is not for us to anticipate God's action. We remain always open to its fulfilment, even when God appears to be silent, no longer 'speaking' his word. We need constancy, determination and resolve in this wilderness experience, trusting in the goodness of God and the wisdom of his word – holding firm, as Mary did, even when her initial *fiat* was finally tested on Calvary, knowing with her that 'nothing will be impossible with God' (Lk 1:37), and rejoicing with her when the Holy Spirit 'comes upon us' in answer to our 'yes'.

---

12. *Saint Thérèse of Lisieux: General Correspondence*, vol 2, Washington, DC: ICS Publications, 1988, Letter 165, p 861.

CHAPTER 1

Praying with Mark

When considering the theme of prayer in the gospels, it is fitting to begin with Mark. As far as we know, this is the earliest of the gospels – at least as we have them. Whether or not there was an original Aramaic gospel of Matthew, which we do not possess and which may have been earlier than Mark, does not concern us here. There is, of course, another advantage in taking Mark's gospel first. It is the shortest of the four – only sixteen chapters. For that reason, Mark is much easier to manage, and to consider as a whole, than any of the other gospels.

With Mark, as with the other three gospels, the theme of prayer is intimately connected with the central insight of the evangelist. At first sight, we may think that Mark, sometimes known as the 'Gospel of Action', does not have a great deal to tell us about prayer; and it is true that Jesus is presented to us by Mark primarily, it would seem, as a great 'Man of Action'. So, first, it is worth taking a brief overview of Mark's teachings on prayer, beginning with the example of Jesus himself.

Jesus at prayer
Jesus often withdraws from the crowd in Mark, sometimes to escape from his enemies, but at other times to refresh himself in solitude (Mk 1:12; 3:7; 6:31; 7:24, 33; 9:2; 10:1). On two occasions, however, Mark tells us explicitly that Jesus went off alone to pray – once early in the ministry (Mk 1:35), after the cure of Simon's mother-in-law; and once again later in the ministry (Mk 6:46), after the multiplication of the loaves and just before Jesus came to his disciples walking on the water. Mark gives us only two examples, then, of the solitary prayer of Jesus.

However, Mark also tells us that, on two other occasions,

Jesus withdraws from the crowds for solitude. He does not tell us explicitly that he withdraws in order to pray. On one of these occasions, before the choice of the Twelve, we are told simply: 'He went up the mountain and called to him those whom he wanted' (Mk 3:13). On the other occasion, after the return of the apostles from their missionary journey, we are told that Jesus invited them to withdraw with himself, to come aside and relax: 'Come away to a deserted place all by yourselves and rest a while' (Mk 6:31). But apart from the importance of solitude, an ideal condition for prayer, the gospel contains lessons, throughout, on the nature and dimensions of prayer.

Teachings on prayer

Mark mentions – at least indirectly – the importance of inner dispositions for prayer. In this gospel, Jesus warns against the prayer of the Scribes and the Pharisees: 'Isaiah prophesied rightly about you hypocrites, as it is written, "This people honours me with their lips, but their hearts are far from me; in vain do they worship me"' (Mk 7:6-7; Is 29:13). Later again in the gospel, he warns about the prayer of the Scribes who only 'for the sake of appearance say long prayers' (Mk 12:40).

Moreover, Mark is at pains to link prayer explicitly with forgiveness: 'Whenever you stand praying,' Jesus tells us, 'forgive, if you have anything against anyone; so that your Father in heaven may also forgive you your trespasses' (Mk 11:25). So, too, he introduces this teaching on prayer and forgiveness with the great assurance of an infallible response to prayer – a lesson of total confidence in God: 'So I tell you, whatever you ask for in prayer, believe that you have received it, and it will be yours' (Mk 11:24). Another time, Mark gives us an important lesson on the link between faith and prayer: 'Truly I tell you, if you say to this mountain, "Be taken up and thrown into the sea," and if you do not doubt in your heart, but believe that what you say will come to pass, it will be done for you' (Mk 11:23). On that occasion, we also find a prophetic, symbolic gesture: Jesus curses the fig tree, and the following day it is seen to have withered (Mk 11:20).

Mark also links the power of prayer with the establishment of the kingdom and the destruction of the power of Satan. After the transfiguration, the disciples confess that they have been unable to drive out one of the devils. So Jesus says to them: 'This kind can come out only through prayer' (Mk 9:29); the addition 'fasting', incidentally, is not in the original text. So, the kingdom of God is established by the power of prayer. This lesson has a special importance for Mark. It is one of the two texts on prayer in Mark which do not have a parallel in the other gospels (Mk 1:35; 9:29).

We note, too, that Mark wedges his scene of the cleansing of the temple (Mk 11:15-19) in between the cursing of the fig tree (Mk 11:14) and the salutary lesson on faith and prayer when the fig tree is seen to have withered (Mk 11:20-24). This scene in the temple also contains a teaching on prayer. Jesus rebukes the money-changers: 'Is it not written, "My house shall be called a house of prayer for all the nations?"' (Mk 11:17). Incidentally, Mark is the only one of the evangelists who includes the phrase 'for all the nations'. It is found in the original text quoted here from Isaiah (Is 56:7). But it is surprising to find it in Mark rather than in Luke (cf Lk 19:46), for example, where we might expect a more universal dimension to the theme of prayer.

We also, in Mark, have this warning of Jesus: 'Beware, keep alert' (Mk 13:33), which is preceded and followed by yet another warning linked explicitly with prayer: 'Pray that it may not be in winter … Keep awake and pray' (Mk 13:18; 14:38). Finally, we have the powerful example of Jesus himself at prayer in the garden: the Gethsemane prayer (Mk 14:32-42), which will be considered in greater detail later.

The originality of Mark?
These lessons, then, make up the entire teaching of Mark on prayer; other than this, there are a few prayers of blessing and thanksgiving by Jesus, with a clear eucharistic import (Mk 6:41; 8:6-7; 14:22-24). Perhaps the most striking thing about this survey is that it reveals only two references to prayer which do not have

parallels in any of the other gospels: the initial reference to the
solitary prayer of Jesus in the first chapter (Mk 1:35); and the
words of Jesus: 'This kind can come out only through prayer'
(Mk 9:29). So, at first sight, there does not seem to be any great
originality about Mark's teaching on prayer. Moreover, he does
not appear to have a great deal to tell us about prayer – at least
not by comparison with the other evangelists.

We have only to compare Mark with Matthew's gospel, for
example, and all its lessons of Jesus on prayer. There we have
the Sermon on the Mount, with its many sayings about prayer
(Mt 6:5-13). Also, we have only to reflect on how Luke links the
prayer of Jesus with the unfolding of the plan of redemption: at
all the peak moments in the establishment of the kingdom, at all
the great turning-points in the unfolding of God's plan of salvation in Luke's gospel, we find Jesus alone at prayer (Lk 3:21;
6:12; 9:18, 28-29; 11:1).[1] Again, we have only to consider John's
gospel: the great priestly prayer (Jn 17), and the teaching on
prayer 'in the name' of Jesus.[2] There is nothing to compare with
all of this in Mark's gospel.

At first sight, it may seem quite strange to discover that Mark
does not even have the Our Father. We find it in Matthew and in
Luke (cf Mt 6:9-13; Lk 11:2-4). But we do not find it in Mark.
Some would say that Mark is writing primarily for a persecuted
church and that his community needed strength and encouragement, not verbal instruction on prayer. But then, we might reasonably counter: what greater support and consolation for any
suffering and persecuted church than the power of prayer, especially the prayer of Jesus himself.

Intimations of the Our Father
Perhaps the real reason why Mark does not have the Our Father
lies deeper: in the very nature of the gospels themselves, in the
way they were written. We have seen that Mark is the first of the

---

1. There is one equivalent in Mark: when Jesus is alone at prayer before
he chooses the Twelve (Mk 3:13; cf Lk 6:12).
2. Cf Jn 14:13-14; 15:16; 16:23-24; cf 15:7; 1 Jn 3:21-22; 5:14-15.

written gospels. In general, it records the earliest strands of the
gospel tradition. However, there do seem to be unmistakable
traces of the Our Father in Mark.[3] The qualification of God as
'Father in heaven' (Mk 11:25), for example, points to a link with
those same words in Matthew's Our Father (Mt 6:9). Mark has
early formulations, we might say, of some of the prayer's petitions: 'Whenever you stand praying, forgive, if you have anything against anyone; so that your Father in heaven may also
forgive you your trespasses' (Mk 11:25; cf Mt 6:12, 14-15; Lk
11:4); and: 'pray that you may not come into the time of trial'
(Mk 14:38; cf Mt 6:13; Lk 11:4). But the Our Father, as we find it
in Matthew and in Luke, probably represents a later development, two distinct forms of the tradition. So, it is not really cor-
rect to speak, as we sometimes do, of Mark omitting the Our
Father. When writing his gospel, he could hardly omit what had
not yet taken shape at the time in the early church tradition. The
surprising thing, then, is not that Mark wrote so little about
prayer: the surprising thing is that he wrote so much about
prayer.

There is a parallel example which sheds some light on Mark's
treatment of prayer: the teaching on Mary. She is almost entirely
absent from the oldest works of the New Testament – the undis-
puted letters of Paul. It is puzzling to discover that Paul never
mentions the name of Mary, not even when he speaks of the
birth of Jesus (cf Gal 4:4). It is yet more startling to find that she
appears only once during the ministry in the first three gospels
(Mk 3:31-35; Mt 12:46-50; Lk 8:19-21). The little that Mark has to
say about her in no way even suggests the later developments
about the mother of God which we find in the infancy narratives
of Matthew and Luke, or in the Cana and Calvary scenes of John

3. On the Our Father, see Joachim Jeremias, *The Prayers of Jesus*, London:
SCM Press, 1967, pp. 82-107; Raymond E Brown SS, 'The Pater Noster
as an Eschatological Prayer', *Theological Studies*, vol 22, 1961. For the
links between the synoptics and John, in relation to the Our Father, see
Raymond E Brown SS, 'Incidents that are Units in the Synoptic Gospels
but Dispersed in St. John', *Catholic Biblical Quarterly*, vol 23, 1961, pp
143-52.

(Jn 2:1-11; 19:25-27) – those rich gospel teachings which developed only later in the early church, and which record so beautifully for us the place of Mary in the plan of redemption.[4]

By comparison with the whole of the New Testament teaching on Mary, then, the teaching of Mark on prayer is itself original. It shows us that only a few decades after the death of Jesus, we have a solid body of teaching on prayer firmly embedded in the gospel tradition. Already in Mark we see how the early church, right from the outset, valued the teaching of Jesus on prayer and reverently contemplated the example of Jesus himself at prayer.

The Suffering Messiah

We are now in a position to link Mark's teaching on prayer, brief as it is, with the central insight of his gospel. Each evangelist has a central insight, a main concern. In the *Dogmatic Constitution on Divine Revelation*, or *Dei Verbum* as it is otherwise known, Vatican II tells us that the gospels were formed in three stages (*DV* 19). In the first stage, we have the ministry of Jesus: his life, his actions, his teaching – all of which reaches a culmination in his passion and resurrection. Then we have the apostolic preaching: in the full light of the passion and resurrection, the apostles adapted the teaching of Jesus to different audiences. This is the second stage: the oral and written tradition. Finally, we have the third stage, that of the evangelists, when the gospels themselves were written.

The council describes the role of the gospels in relation to the apostolic preaching by saying that each evangelist selects, synthesises and explicates. The word in the original text for 'explicate' is *'explanare'* – a Latin term meaning 'to draw out', 'to expand' or 'to develop'. The evangelist does all this – selects, synthesises, explicates – with a view to his main concern, his central

---

4. For an extensive treatment of the development in the understanding of Mary's place in the early Christian community, see Raymond E Brown SS, 'Mary in the New Testament and in Catholic Life', *America*, 15 May 1982, pp 374-9; see, too, James McCaffrey OCD, 'Discovering Mary with the Gospels', *Mount Carmel*, vol 48/1, 2000, pp 43-8, and the section 'Discovering the mystery of Mary' in the Epilogue to this book.

insight. And it seems to be the main concern of Mark to present Jesus as the Suffering Messiah (cf Is 52:13-53:12). This is not to say that Jesus is the Suffering Messiah in Mark's gospel alone. But this is Mark's central insight, his main concern. In his gospel, Jesus stands alone and misunderstood. He is not understood by his disciples or even by Peter; he is not understood by his relatives; and he is certainly not understood by his enemies. Mark emphasises this failure to understand; and he stresses, likewise, the suffering of Jesus.

The 'Messianic Secret'

The entire gospel of Mark seems to pivot around this central insight. We have only to recall his use of what is known as the 'Messianic Secret': Jesus concealing his identity as the Messiah. Throughout Mark's gospel, he works miracles. Yet almost invariably he tells the people, and sometimes even the demons themselves, not to talk about them. This is indeed strange. It is almost like telling them not to accept him. Yet his entire life is a plea for acceptance.

Already in the very first chapter of the gospel, we have the cure of a man with an unclean spirit. The demon says: 'I know who you are, the Holy One of God' (Mk 1:24). But Jesus rebukes him, saying: 'Be silent, and come out of him!' (Mk 1:25). Still in that first chapter, we have a series of miracles, or cures. There again we read the words of Jesus to a leper who has just been healed: 'See that you say nothing to anyone' (Mk 1:44). So we can just imagine how Mark has tongue in cheek, telling us that the leper went off after the cure 'and began to proclaim it freely, and to spread the word' (Mk 1:45). Later in the gospel, the demons again cry out: 'You are the Son of God!' (Mk 3:11). Jesus, we are told, 'sternly ordered them not to make him known' (Mk 3:12). The same is true again after the cure of the daughter of Jairus when Jesus speaks to a few privileged witnesses: 'He strictly ordered them that no one should know this' (Mk 5:43; cf 1:34; 7:36; 8:26; 9:9).

These are only a few examples of the 'Messianic Secret'. They by no means exhaust Mark's use of it. But even when we come to the great turning-point in Mark's gospel, the scene at Caesarea Philippi with Peter's profession of faith, we are told that there, too, 'he sternly ordered them not to tell anyone about him' (Mk 8:30). There must be no mistake. Jesus is not to be the popular hero, the great wonder-worker, the victorious Messiah of Jewish expectations. He is to be the Suffering Messiah.

Style is the man

We say that style is the man. This is also true of the evangelists. In Mark, the language itself – his style – is continually pressed into service to drive home that one central insight of his gospel. Mark's style is rough, abrupt, awkward – even more noticeably so in the original Greek text; this jarring tone bears the obvious traces of oral improvisation.[5] The evangelist also seems to play on the emotions, as he alone records how Jesus embraced a child, 'taking it in his arms' (Mk 9:36; cf Mt 19:13; Lk 18:15). The pictorial quality of the style is striking, too. It is Mark alone who adds a telling detail to his description of the storm on the lake, when he informs us that Jesus was 'asleep on the cushion' (Mk 4:38; cf Mt 8:24; Lk 8:23). Mark also likes to heighten the dramatic effect of his narrative, as we experience through his eyes how a blind man comes only gradually to full vision (Mk 8:22-26). It is hardly surprising that it was Mark, rather than any of the other evangelists, who provided a modern actor, Alec McGowan, with the text for his one-man television and stage presentation of the gospel story.

It is often said that Mark's gospel is, more than the others, the gospel of proclamation, the 'kerygmatic' gospel. What it proclaims is the bald facts, indeed the disconcerting facts – the contradiction, rejection and misunderstanding of Jesus, his loneliness, weakness and failures. It is all part of that terrible realism of Mark's gospel. We talk about the starkness of Mark. He is not

---

5. On the style of the evangelists, see Albert Vanhoye SJ, *Structure and Theology of the Accounts of the Passion in the Synoptic Gospels*, Collegeville, MN: The Liturgical Press, 1967, pp 8-10.

afraid to startle us, to scare us, to stun us, to jog us out of our complacency and to disturb us.[6] He plunges us into the darkness of human weakness and human suffering and underlines the paradox that the cross is the scandal which reveals the Son of God. The result is an act of faith – light in the darkness. It requires submission to the mystery: that Jesus saves through suffering.

Even the whole thrust of Mark's gospel, emerging ever more clearly as the ministry of Jesus unfolds, is a movement out of darkness into light. We see this illustrated beautifully for us in one of the parables of Jesus. It is found only in Mark (Mk 4:26-29), so it clearly has a special significance for him. It tells how the seed sprouts and grows in the depths of the earth, without the sower being aware of it. It edges its way, imperceptibly, towards the light while 'the earth produces of itself, first the stalk, then the head, then the full grain in the head' (Mk 4:28). Mark's good news has rightly been called 'a gospel of veiled epiphanies' – shrouded in general darkness but at the same time filled with revelations and manifestations of light. Even in moments of thickest darkness, brightness always seems to shimmer through.

The turning-point

The whole structure of Mark shows how his gospel pivots around its central insight. The first part asks a number of questions but without giving the answers. In the first chapter, immediately after Jesus has cured a man with an unclean spirit, we read: 'They were all amazed, and they kept on asking one another, "What is this? A new teaching – with authority! He commands even the unclean spirits, and they obey him"' (Mk 1:27). But no answer is given.

This same pattern continues throughout the following chapters. We have the cure of the paralytic in the second chapter.

---

6. We find a parallel to the stark realism of Mark's approach in some of the modern, realistic Stations of the Cross; a striking example is the 'Golgotha of Jasna Gora' by the Polish artist Jerzy Duda Gracz in Czestochowa.

Some people bring him to Jesus and let him down through an opening in the roof. Then Mark tells us, 'Now some of the scribes were sitting there, questioning in their hearts ... "It is blasphemy! Who can forgive sins but God alone?"... and he said to them, "Why do you raise such questions in your hearts?"' (Mk 2:6-8). Questions again, but without any answers.

Then we have a list of miracles. The first one highlights a great moment in the gospel (Mk 4:35-41). It is when Jesus calms the sea: 'Peace! Be still!' he says (Mk 4:39). The climax of that story comes again with a question: 'Who then is this, that even the wind and the sea obey him?' (Mk 4:41). But again no answer is given. On yet another occasion, Jesus comes to his own home town. Mark tells us that the people of Nazareth are astonished: 'Where did this man get all this?' they ask. 'What is this wisdom that has been given to him? What deeds of power are being done by his hands! Is not this the carpenter, the son of Mary?' (Mk 6:2-3). More questions. Again no answers.

So, all through the first part of Mark's gospel, we have questions. And we note that they all have something in common: they are questions about the identity of Jesus. Who is he? We are left in suspense, waiting for an answer. Then comes the great turning-point in the gospel, the scene at Caesarea Philippi (Mk 8:27-30). This time it is Jesus who asks the questions: 'Who do people say that I am?' he begins. They answer him, 'John the Baptist; and others, Elijah; and still others, one of the prophets.' Then Jesus asks, 'But who do *you* say that I am?' And Peter answers, 'You are the Messiah.' We notice again the 'Messianic Secret': 'He sternly ordered them not to tell anyone about him.' Yes, Jesus is the Messiah. But not the victorious Messiah of Jewish expectations, not the Messiah the Jews were hoping him to be. Jesus now reveals that he is to be the Suffering Messiah.

Dying and rising with Jesus
At this same turning-point, we have the first prediction of the passion and resurrection in Mark:

Then he began to teach them that the Son of Man must undergo great suffering, and be rejected by the elders, the chief priests, and the scribes, and be killed, and after three days rise again. He said all this quite openly. (Mk 8:31-32)

Mark will arrange the entire second part of his gospel around three predictions of the passion and resurrection. It is very easy to remember them, spaced apart as they are at almost the same distance (Mk 8:31-32; 9:31-32; 10:33-34). The evangelist follows the same pattern each time: first the prediction and then mis-understanding.

After the first prediction, Peter takes Jesus aside and begins to remonstrate with him. Then Jesus, we are told, looks round, sees the other disciples and rebukes Peter: 'Get behind me, Satan! For you are setting your mind not on divine things but on human things' (Mk 8:33). After the second prediction, Mark tells us explicitly: 'They did not understand what he was saying and were afraid to ask him' (Mk 9:32). Finally, after the third predic-tion, we are told the story of the sons of Zebedee coming to Jesus and asking him 'to sit, one at your right hand and one at your left, in your glory' (Mk 10:37). Again, total misunderstanding. The passion and resurrection of Jesus is a mystery which baffles the human mind.

It is within the framework of that triple prediction of the passion and resurrection that Mark gives us his teaching on dis-cipleship. After the first prediction, we hear the words: 'If any want to become my followers, let them deny themselves and take up their cross and follow me. For those who want to save their life will lose it, and those who lose their life for my sake, and for the sake of the gospel, will save it' (Mk 8:34-35). After the second prediction, we are told that Jesus turns to his disciples and asks, 'What were you arguing about on the way?' (Mk 9:33). There is a momentary pause. 'They were silent,' Mark tells us, and adds that they were arguing about 'who was the greatest' (Mk 9:34). Then Jesus takes a little child and sets the child in their midst. There, he says to them with this eloquent gesture, you have true greatness. When, after the third prediction, we find the sons of Zebedee asking for the places of honour in the

kingdom, Jesus replies, 'Are you able to drink the cup ... be baptised with the baptism that I am baptised with?' (Mk 10:38).
Immediately, he gives us his great lesson on discipleship: 'For
the Son of man came not to be served but to serve, and to give
his life as a ransom for many' (Mk 10:45) – total service unto
death.

It is the same road for every follower of Jesus, the way of
Jesus himself through his passion and death to the resurrection –
a dying and a rising. It is the way of the paschal mystery,
through the darkness to the light.

A journey of faith

This is the journey of faith in Mark – out of the darkness into the
light. Significantly, he introduces this ascent of Jesus to
Jerusalem – to his passion and resurrection – with the story of
the cure of a blind man (Mk 8:22-26). He ends this journey with
the cure of another blind man: Bartimaeus, the blind beggar (Mk
10:46-52). Both these stories illustrate the movement of faith in
Mark's gospel. Consider the description of the first of these
cures:

> They came to Bethsaida. Some people brought a blind man to
> him and begged him to touch him. He took the blind man by
> the hand and led him out of the village; and when he had put
> saliva on his eyes and laid his hands on him, he asked him,
> 'Can you see anything?' And the man looked up and said, 'I
> can see people, but they look like trees, walking.' Then Jesus
> laid his hands on his eyes again; and he looked intently and
> his sight was restored, and he saw everything clearly. Then
> he sent him away to his home, saying, 'Do not even go into
> the village.' (Mk 8:22-26)

Note that this is a miracle in slow motion. We see the blind
man groping his way out of the darkness into the light. But
things are still blurred, not yet in focus, until finally he comes
gradually to clear vision. Out of the darkness into the light – a
meaningful image of faith in Mark's gospel. We will return later

to consider in detail the cure of Bartimaeus at the end of Jesus' journey to Jerusalem. But we should keep in mind, for the moment, the last verse in that story: 'Jesus said to him, "Go; your faith has made you well." Immediately he regained his sight and followed him on the way' (Mk 10:52). On the way! Jesus is 'on the way' to his passion, his death and his resurrection. Here again, we have an image of faith and of the paschal mystery at the heart of discipleship in Mark.

These two miracles illustrate the whole movement of Mark's gospel where light shimmers through even in the thickest darkness. This also illustrates the journey of faith as a continual groping through the night towards the first streaks of dawn. It is a following of Jesus along the way of his dying and his rising.

The power of faith

We might look now for a moment at some of the qualities of faith in Mark. We have already learnt something about faith in the story of Bartimaeus who, once cured from blindness, follows Jesus 'on the way' to the passion, death and resurrection. To believe is to adhere to a person – the person of Jesus, the crucified and risen Saviour – and to follow him on the way of his dying and rising again.

We see another quality of faith in Mark, when Jesus says to his disciples, 'Have faith in God' (Mk 11:22). That is how the words are usually translated. They stress that God himself – and not just articles of belief – is the object of faith. And so he is. But what Mark says in the original text may well have an added richness of meaning. He is literally saying, 'Have the faith of God' – that is, faith which is a gift of God. Faith, then, is a free gift. We should not overlook the fuller possibilities of this phrase.

Mark uses vivid imagery when he speaks of faith: 'Truly I tell you, if you say to this mountain, "Be taken up and thrown into the sea," and if you do not doubt in your heart, but believe that what you say will come to pass, it will be done for you' (Mk 11:23). Matthew, too, speaks of faith that can move mountains

(Mt 17:20). The expression must have been deeply embedded in the early tradition. We seem to have an echo of it in Paul as well, when he too speaks of a faith that is able to move mountains (cf 1 Cor 13:2). Faith can achieve the impossible. The words of Mark also describe how, through the prayer of faith, the impossible becomes possible: 'So I tell you, whatever you ask for in prayer, believe that you have received it, and it will be yours' (Mk 11:24). What Mark wrote is in the past tense: 'you have received'. An assurance indeed of an infallible response to the prayer of faith. The believer is challenged to an unshakable trust in the power of God when all else fails. By faith, we share in the power of God himself: 'for God all things are possible' (Mk 10:27; cf Lk 1:37).

Another of Mark's gospel stories gives a beautiful illustration of the power of faith. It is the cure of the woman with the issue of blood (Mk 5:25-34). We see her edging her way through the crowd into the presence of Jesus just to touch the hem of his garments. And she is cured: 'Immediately her haemorrhage stopped' (Mk 5:29). Power, we are told, went out from Jesus. The story ends with the words: 'Your faith has made you well; go in peace' (Mk 5:34). Faith heals, and it draws forth the power of God. It makes us receptive, open to his action, his powerful healing action.

Waiting on the Lord
There is one other quality of faith which is called for, when Mark records the warning of Jesus: 'Be alert' (Mk 13:23). The warning prepares the believer for future obstacles, trials and difficulties, the 'tribulation' at the end of time (Mk 13:19-23). Faith will be tested. So, Jesus calls for a determined and persevering prayer of faith: 'Beware, keep alert' (Mk 13:33).

We find a strange paradox at the heart of Christian prayer. We are continually on the move forward, a pilgrim church; and still we are always waiting, always expecting, always attentive and watching. In a real sense, God is always with us; God is always in our midst. But also, in a real sense, he is the God beyond, the God who has yet to come. So we wait and watch, expectantly. This is one of the many telling lessons which we can learn from the apparitions of the risen Jesus, such as the story of the disciples on the road to Emmaus: 'Then their eyes were opened, and they recognised him; and he vanished from their sight' (Lk 24:31). Just at the moment when they recognise him in the breaking of the bread, he suddenly disappears. The disciples discover him, only to lose him again. The same lesson is given to us in the story of Jacob wrestling with the Unknown Stranger, grappling with him in the night (Gen 32:22-32). The Stranger withdraws continually, receding into the darkness.

In prayer, we discover God when we persevere in the struggle. But we discover him, only to lose him again. To pray is to journey towards a God of the unexpected who is always new, always different and yet always the same. Each step of the journey tells us something more about him, as he recedes continually into the darkness of his own mystery. It is a voyage of perpetual beginnings, a continual discovery full of new surprises. But we must wait on God's moment of light, his revelation. We must watch 'more than watchman for daybreak' (Ps 129:6). We watch and wait, patiently – with a determined and persevering faith. It is this aspect of Christian prayer that is so well summed up for us in the prayer of the early church: 'Come, Lord Jesus!' (Rev 22:20; cf 1 Cor 16:22).

Into the light
In Mark, faith and prayer are inseparable. In one of his most important teachings on faith, Mark links it explicitly with the theme of prayer. This is the passage:

> Have faith in God. Truly I tell you, if you say to this mountain, 'Be taken up and thrown into the sea,' and if you do not doubt in your heart, but believe that what you say will come to pass, it will be done for you. So I tell you, whatever you ask for in prayer, believe that you have received it, and it will be yours. (Mk 11:22-24)

When Mark links prayer and faith in the story of Bartimaeus (Mk 10:46-52), we have not just this trust and confidence but many other dimensions of Mark's teachings on faith. We are told that Bartimaeus is a blind beggar – blind, sightless, in the dark. A beggar in need. Apparently, there is no human remedy for his affliction (cf Mk 5:26). But we are told that Jesus is passing, so there is a chance for an encounter with Jesus. That is what prayer is: an encounter with Jesus, a meeting with him. Out of the darkness of his own weakness, Bartimaeus cries for help. It is a cry of faith: 'Jesus, Son of David, have mercy on me!' (Mk 10:47). There, out of the darkness comes the light. We notice, though, that Bartimaeus also has a determined and persevering faith. He will not be discouraged in his efforts. Many of the by-standers, we are told, rebuke him, telling him to be silent. But 'he cried out even more loudly, "Son of David, have mercy on me!"' (Mk 10:48). Jesus stops and calls him, finding him, discovering him in his need. And Jesus says, 'What do you want me to do for you?' (Mk 10:51). The blind man replies, 'My teacher, let me see again' (Mk 10:51) – a cry for light in the darkness. Jesus says to him, 'Go; your faith has made you well' (Mk 10:52). Immediately, the man regains his sight and follows him 'on the way' – which, as we have seen, also means the 'way' of the passion, death and resurrection. Bartimaeus is drawn out of his human misery and weakness, out of the darkness and into the light.

The solitary Jesus

If we look more closely at the times when Jesus withdraws from the crowd, we will see how his moments of solitude are linked with the central insight and paradox of his gospel: Jesus as the Suffering Messiah. As mentioned earlier, there are two occasions when Mark shows Jesus withdrawing from the crowd but does not tell us explicitly that he goes away to pray.

The first of these, as we have seen, occurs just before Jesus chooses the twelve apostles: 'He went up the mountain,' we are told, 'and called to him those whom he wanted, and they came to him. And he appointed twelve' (Mk 3:13-14) – literally, what Mark says is that 'he made twelve' (*epoiêsan*). His call is a creative act. He constitutes them as the 'Twelve': 'to be with him, and to be sent out to proclaim the message' (Mk 3:14). But we notice that Mark first presents Jesus to us here as a popular hero and great wonder-worker: 'Jesus departed with his disciples to the sea,' we are told, 'and a great multitude from Galilee followed him ... they came to him in great numbers from Judea, Jerusalem, Idumea, beyond the Jordan, and the region around Tyre and Sidon' – a great multitude ... in great numbers – and, we are told, 'he had cured many' (Mk 3:7-8, 10).

Then Mark reminds us, in his own subtle way, that Jesus has not come to be the great wonder-worker or popular hero. The 'Messianic Secret' rings out immediately, loud and clear: 'He sternly ordered them not to make him known' (Mk 3:12). At this precise moment, Mark tells us that Jesus withdraws into the hills: 'He went up the mountain' (Mk 3:13). Jesus seems at times to feel the need to withdraw for quiet during his ministry, even – and especially – when he appears to be most successful. The miracles of Jesus are his acts of power. But here, right at the heart of his saving mission, at the moment when Jesus is most accepted and, apparently, most powerful, Mark directs us away from those miracles to the real source of his power. Solitude, it would seem, is the hidden spring of his saving work. Mark tells us that Jesus withdraws in order to be alone. In these quiet moments away from the crowd, his saving mission cannot be far from his mind. It is surely significant that Jesus spends time in solitude and silence before creating his new community on the firm foundation of the Twelve.

We should notice also the wider context of the scene. Mark introduces it with several short episodes, each of them showing Jesus in controversy with his enemies. In the last one, Mark opens up for us, in no uncertain terms, the perspective of the death of Jesus: 'The Pharisees went out,' we are told, 'and immediately conspired with the Herodians against him, how to destroy him' (Mk 3:6). Still in that wider context, Mark highlights the refusal of the enemies of Jesus to understand, as well as their lack of faith. Jesus, he tells us, 'looked around at them with anger; he was grieved at their hardness of heart' (Mk 3:5). Here we have misunderstanding, unbelief, and even the perspective of the death of Jesus – and all of this accentuated by contrast with popular acceptance and acclaim. So it is not surprising that we see Jesus during his ministry impelled, as it were, into solitude, to refresh his mind at the hidden spring of his saving power. Jesus in solitude seems to be plunged into darkness, immersed in the mystery of his mission to save through suffering and failure.

An invitation to solitude

As mentioned previously, there is one other time when Jesus withdraws from the crowd in Mark without any explicit mention of withdrawing in order to pray. On this occasion, Jesus invites his disciples to withdraw with him: 'He said to them, "Come away to a deserted place all by yourselves and rest a while." For many were coming and going, and they had no leisure even to eat. And they went away in the boat to a deserted place by themselves' (Mk 6:31-32). In this scene, the disciples are clearly the victims of popular demand (cf Mk 1:37). They are busy, possibly even too busy, with the spread of the kingdom.

Again, we should notice the wider context of the scene. A few verses previously, we are told that Jesus has come to his own country. There, Mark describes the effect of his return: 'And they took offence at him … And he was amazed at their unbelief' (Mk 6:3, 6). The evangelist reminds us once again of the same basic response to Jesus: misunderstanding and unbelief. This danger is always present in Mark's gospel.

Jesus invites the Twelve to withdraw into solitude just after they return from their mission. Mark describes the success of their endeavours in clear terms: 'They cast out many demons, and anointed with oil many who were sick and cured them' (Mk 6:13). In this chapter, the evangelist uses what is called, somewhat inelegantly, a sandwich technique: there, wedged between the sending out and the return, we have the story of the death of John the Baptist (Mk 6:14-29).

We should listen carefully to Mark's description. He first describes Herod's reaction to the mission of the apostles and to Jesus himself: 'John the baptiser,' he tells us, 'has been raised from the dead' (Mk 6:14). Mark even describes Herod's reaction a second time, again in similar terms: 'John, whom I beheaded, has been raised' (Mk 6:16). Then comes the climax to the story: 'When the disciples heard about it, they came and took his body, and laid it in a tomb' (Mk 6:29; cf 15:46). The evangelist clearly describes the entire scene with an eye to the future passion, death and resurrection of Jesus.

This context, then, speaks once more of death and resurrection, and misunderstanding, again heightened by contrast with popular success and acclaim. And, as we have seen, Jesus here invites his apostles to withdraw, to come away into solitude and silence to reflect. To ponder, it would seem, on the meaning of their saving mission. There must be no mistake. The mission of the apostles, like that of the Baptist and like the mission of Jesus himself, is a dying and a rising. Again, we touch on the central paradox of Mark's gospel: light out of darkness, redemption through suffering and death.

Jesus alone at prayer

Now we might look more closely at another episode where we are told that Jesus withdraws from the crowd. This time, however, we are told explicitly that he has withdrawn in order to pray. The incident occurs immediately after the multiplication of the loaves (Mk 6:34-44). So Mark presents Jesus to us again as the great wonder-worker, the popular hero. Jesus then 'went up on the mountain to pray' (Mk 6:46). Afterwards, he emerges out of that prayer and comes to his disciples, walking on the waters. But we notice how the evangelist concludes his description of the scene. He directs our attention back to the miracle of the loaves just before Jesus enters into prayer; and he describes the reaction of the disciples to the miracle: 'They did not understand about the loaves, but their hearts were hardened' (Mk 6:52). Jesus again comes face to face with failure in his mission, and encounters the darkness of human understanding, the response of unbelief.

But after this great miracle of the loaves which the disciples fail to understand, we see Jesus emerging from his prayer in the 'evening' (Mk 6:47) and appearing to his disciples walking on the water just before dawn (Mk 6:48). He comes to them with a great self-revelation: 'Take heart, it is I; do not be afraid' (Mk 6:50). Out of the darkness comes a great moment of light![7]

Wasting time in prayer?

Finally, there is one other important episode to consider in Mark, where we are again told explicitly that Jesus withdraws to pray. The scene has a special significance. It occurs in the opening chapter of Mark and is, in fact, the first occasion in his gospel where we are told that Jesus withdraws to pray (Mk 1:35). It does not have a parallel in the other gospels: Mark is the only evangelist who tells us that Jesus at this point in his ministry goes off alone to pray. Moreover, this solitary prayer of Jesus is not intended as an isolated incident but as an integral part of a typical day in Jesus' ministry. The whole section of the gospel where it occurs is highly structured (Mk 1:21-45).[8] It is composed of several closely-knit episodes in his ministry of teaching and healing throughout the day (Mk 1:21-28, 29-31, 32-34, 35-39, 40-45). Here, the evangelist intends to give us a picture of a typical day in the early ministry of Jesus. It represents any day in the life of Jesus.

In this episode, we see Jesus stealing off before dawn: 'In the morning, while it was still very dark, he got up and went out to a deserted place, and there he prayed' (Mk 1:35). At this time of

---

7. 'Ego eimi' ('I am') in the original text points to the divine nature of Jesus (cf Ex 3:14).
8. 'This section [Mk 1:21-34] ... is intended to give a typical picture of the early ministry.': see Wilfrid Harrington OP, *Mark*, Dublin: Veritas (New Testament Message, vol 4), 1979, p 15.

day, we might think that Jesus can reasonably expect to be left alone to commune with his Father, free from interruptions and the pressure of his ministry. But that is not to be. Once again, the evangelist draws a veil over the content of the prayer of Jesus. We are asked to respect the mystery. But the context itself is eloquent. The same basic pattern occurs. Just before Jesus goes away to pray, Mark presents him to us as the popular hero, the great wonder-worker: 'And the whole city was gathered around the door,' we are told. 'And he cured many who were sick with various diseases, and cast out many demons' (Mk 1:33-34). The kingdom of God has come with great acts of power. Here again we find the 'Messianic Secret': 'He would not permit the demons to speak, because they knew him' (Mk 1:34). Jesus is *not* to be the popular hero, not even the great wonder-worker. He is the Suffering Messiah, who will establish the kingdom through his sufferings and the power of his prayer.

We notice again how Mark brings out the failure of Jesus and the misunderstanding of the disciples: 'Simon and his companions hunted for him' (Mk 1:36), encroaching even on his solitary prayer, and 'when they found him, they said to him, "Everyone is searching for you"' (Mk 1:37). By their standards – human standards – Jesus is an unqualified success, so the disciples go after him. The translation, 'hunted for him', hardly captures the full force of the original text: *katediôxen* is a word used to describe a victorious army in relentless pursuit of the vanquished.

The disciples cannot see any reason for this quiet prayer in the life of Jesus when there are so many pressing demands on him. It appears useless, without value, a waste of time. For them, it obviously has no place in his ministry, in his service of the world at large. They fail to understand that prayer is the hidden spring, the sustaining and indispensable power behind the mission of Jesus. So they pursue him ceaselessly, trying pitilessly to draw him away from his quiet communion with his Father, away to embrace popularity and human success: 'Everyone is searching for you' (Mk 1:37). Significantly, in that quiet time of prayer, away from the crowd, his saving mission is not far from the mind of Jesus. It is hardly accidental that he speaks of it again immediately after his prayer. He says to his disciples – almost in desperation, it would seem! – 'Let us go on to the neighbouring towns, so that I may proclaim the message there also; for that is what I came out to do' (Mk 1:38).

In all of these episodes, we find the same basic lessons. Jesus has come to establish the kingdom. His miracles are his acts of power and they are greeted with popular acclaim. Jesus is a powerful 'Man of Action' in Mark. But the same evangelist reminds us continually that he is not just a wonder-worker. He is no mere popular hero. He is the Suffering Messiah, although people just will not understand. We see Jesus impelled almost by this mystery of human weakness and misunderstanding, by the mystery of unbelief, by his own failure and rejection and sufferings – impelled into solitude and prayer to steep his mind in the darkness of the mystery. But it is through the power of that prayer that the kingdom of God is realised (Mk 9:29). Out of that prayer comes redemption, out of that darkness comes the light, out of that suffering and failure comes the gift of faith, eternal life.

Gethsemane prayer

The whole of Mark's teaching on prayer is exemplified in his portrayal of Jesus at prayer in Gethsemane (Mk 14:32-42).[9] Here, the evangelist is at pains to underline for us the weakness of Jesus, his sheer physical exhaustion in the garden. He tells us that Jesus falls on the ground. But the word that he uses describes a repeated action: it implies that he keeps on falling, again and again. Mark also tells us that Jesus 'began to be distressed and agitated. And he said to them, "I am deeply grieved, even to death"' (Mk 14:33-34). Jesus is seized with horror and distress. The New English Bible captures well his strong emotions at prayer, his surprise and terror and grief. It translates

9. For a comprehensive study of the Gethsemane prayer, see David M Stanley SJ, *Jesus in Gethsemane: The Early Church Reflects on the Suffering of Jesus*, New York & Ramsey, NJ: Paulist Press, 1980.

them with these words: 'Horror and dismay came over him, and he said to them, "My heart is ready to break with grief".'

However, the original language of Mark is even more graphic: Jesus begins to be 'utterly dismayed' – the '*ekthambeisthai*' of the original has the crushing impact of a sudden clap of thunder – and, literally, 'to be out of his mind' ('*adêmoneô*') with grief. Still his disciples fail to understand. Jesus finds them asleep: 'The spirit indeed is willing,' we are reminded, 'but the flesh is weak' (Mk 14:38). We are then told that Jesus again left his disciples 'and prayed, saying the same words' (Mk 14:39). 'The same words' can undoubtedly refer to the previous prayer of Jesus: 'Abba, Father, for you all things are possible; remove this cup from me; yet, not what I want, but what you want' (Mk 14:36). But not necessarily so. These 'words' can also be a prayer referring directly to what he has just said previously: 'The spirit indeed is willing, but the flesh is weak' (Mk 14:38) – something which Jesus himself was experiencing while at prayer.[10] He has warned his disciples at the outset: 'Remain here, and keep awake' (Mk 14:34). Now, he warns them again: 'Keep awake' (Mk 14:38). But this time he adds the word 'pray': 'Keep awake and pray that you may not come into the time of trial' (Mk 14:38). Keep on watching, keep on praying. Jesus himself, at prayer in the garden of Gethsemane, gives the example. For the disciple of Jesus, there will be a time of testing. Determination will be needed, strength for the battle. Survival is the fruit of persevering prayer.

Mark also stresses the loneliness of Jesus, his deep need for human companionship. We may remember that Jesus withdraws from his disciples three times in that scene and returns to them again three times. Matthew stresses the fact that Jesus

---

10. Stanley observes: 'Usually, *the same words* are understood to refer to the articulated prayer in v. 36, and Jesus is thought to repeat the petition he had already made to be released by the Father from the drinking of *this cup*. While this is, of course, not implausible, I venture to suggest that he now prays to God about the human dilemma, which he has just voiced: *The spirit indeed is willing, yet the flesh is weak*. Jesus … has realized his own weakness.' See Stanley, *op. cit.*, p 143.

withdraws from the disciples. Mark does not tell us, at least not explicitly, that Jesus goes away three times, but he does stress the fact that he *returns* three times (Mk 14:37, 40, 41). Jesus – in his prayer, in his anguish – not only needs the companionship of his disciples but also is still the caring Shepherd of his flock (Mk 14:27).

Moreover, Jesus prays not just once, but over and over again 'that, if it were possible, the hour might pass from him'. He says, 'Abba, Father, for you all things are possible; remove this cup from me; yet, not what I want, but what you want' (Mk 14:35-36). He means it. The 'cup' is the chalice of total failure. The one thing that Jesus has come to accomplish is to unite and gather around himself a community. Yet the one effect of his passion and his death will be to scatter that very community: 'I will strike the shepherd, and the sheep will be scattered' (Mk 14:27; Zech 13:7). But Jesus struggles in prayer through darkness and human weakness to discover the light of God's will: 'yet, not what I want, but what you want' (Mk 14:36). It is a real battle for Jesus to discover God's will and to surrender to it. He does it in the desolation of darkness; and finally he submits. There is no acting, no pretence.

Calvary anticipated

The scene in the garden foreshadows the lesson of Calvary. As Jesus hung on the cross, we are told:

> When it was noon, darkness came over the whole land until three in the afternoon. At three o'clock Jesus cried out with a loud voice, 'Eloi, Eloi, lema sabachthani?' which means, 'My God, my God, why have you forsaken me?' (Mk 15:33-34)

The inner failure, abandonment and anguish of the soul of Jesus are reflected in the external darkness. But out of the inner darkness comes the light: 'Truly this man was God's Son!' (Mk 15:39) – a cry of faith on the lips of a pagan who was serving as a centurion in the imperial army of Rome. This is again a fitting climax to the gospel of Mark, with its central insight that Jesus is the Suffering Messiah, and its pervading paradox: light in darkness.

Perhaps nobody has ever described this central paradox of Mark's gospel better than John of the Cross. It provided him with the pattern of prayer in the darkest moments of spiritual growth. In *The Ascent of Mount Carmel*, he comments on the words, 'My God, my God, why have you forsaken me?' (Mk 15:34):

> This was the most extreme abandonment, sensitively, that he had suffered in his life. And by it he accomplished the most marvellous work of his whole life ... the reconciliation and union of the human race with God through grace. The Lord achieved this ... that those who are truly spiritual might understand the mystery of the door and way (which is Christ) leading to union with God ... When they are reduced to nothing, the highest degree of humility, the spiritual union between their souls and God will be an accomplished fact. (2A:7:11)

And others, too, perhaps even unknowingly, are groping along this same way to the light, finding a way out of evil and pain, the ache of silence and loneliness, towards a meaning for life. Petru Dumitriu describes his own spiritual odyssey in these words:

> Perhaps I am going to climb and crawl, right up to the last instant, towards that unknown hearth of radiant brightness, drag myself on hands and knees towards God, doubt in my heart and ignorance in my numbskull brain ... hoping for I know not what ... going towards him without knowing where he is nor who he is.[11]

Finally, for Karl Rahner, this journey through darkness to the light is the way of authentic prayer. He calls it our sharing,

11. Petru Dumitriu, *To the Unknown God*, New York: Seabury Press, 1982, p 244.

through the Spirit, in the 'cup' or chalice of Christ, which is a gateway from desolation to the life of grace:

> The chalice of the Holy Spirit is identical in this life with the chalice of Christ. This chalice is drunk only by those who have slowly learned in little ways to taste the fullness in emptiness, the ascent in the fall, life in death, the finding in renunciation. Anyone who learns this, experiences the spirit – the pure spirit – and in this experience he is also given the experience of the Holy Spirit of grace.[12]

12. Karl Rahner SJ, 'Reflections on the Experience of Grace', in his *Theological Investigations*, vol III: *The Theology of the Spiritual Life*, London: DLT/New York: Seabury Press, 1974, p 89.

For Pondering and Prayer

1. Church teaching in *Dei Verbum* (*Dogmatic Constitution on Divine Revelation*) #19 distinguishes three stages in the formation of the gospels. In what way can this be helpful as an approach to the gospels?

2. The themes of light and darkness pervade the gospel of Mark. How is this linked with his teaching on the prayer of faith?

3. Mark, more than any of the other evangelists, stresses the humanity of Jesus and the weakness of the disciples. Does this help us to understand better Mark's treatment of prayer?

A GUIDED *LECTIO DIVINA*

The rich young man (Mk 10:17-22)

As [Jesus] was setting out on a journey, a man ran up and knelt before him, and asked him, 'Good Teacher, what must I do to inherit eternal life?' Jesus said to him, 'Why do you call me good? No one is good but God alone. You know the commandments: "You shall not murder; You shall not commit adultery; You shall not steal; You shall not bear false witness; You shall not defraud; Honour your father and mother".' He said to him, 'Teacher, I have kept all these since my youth.' Jesus, looking at him, loved him and said, 'You lack one thing; [Mt 19:21: 'If you wish to be perfect...] go, sell what you own, and give the money to the poor, and you will have treasure in heaven; then come, follow me.' When he heard this, he was shocked and went away grieving, for he had many possessions.

Reading

Relax. Invoke the Holy Spirit. Then read this passage slowly, attentively and reverently, with mind and heart open to receive the word, ready to respond to whatever it asks of you. Know that it is a word of love from God addressed to you personally. Reread it two or three times – calmly, quietly and without haste.

Meditation

Take any word or phrase that strikes you spontaneously. For example: 'If you wish to be perfect ...' Reflect on the word 'perfect'. Are you at ease with it, or does it disturb and frighten you? Ponder on your reaction and give reasons for it. Recall another use of this word in the gospel. For example: 'Be perfect, therefore, as your heavenly Father is perfect' (Mt 5:48). How does this help you to understand the notion of 'perfection'?

Look at the man's reaction: 'He was shocked and went away grieving, for he had many possessions.' Does this remind you of any similar experience in your own life? Do you remember an occasion in the gospels when others rejected the love of Jesus? For example: 'many of his disciples turned back and no longer went about with him' (Jn 6:66). Again, consider your own reaction.

Prayer

Jesus looked at the rich young man with 'love'. Know that he is looking at you in the same way. Let your heart go out freely, answering with love. You might say something like this: 'Jesus, I thank you for loving me. Have pity on me. Help me not to turn away from your invitation. Give me the courage always to say "yes" to you.'

Contemplation

Remain in the presence of Jesus with your mind still, looking at him who is looking at you, his eyes brimming with love and mercy. Let the silence deepen, ignoring distractions that threaten your quiet gaze of love in response to his. Stay in the silence, rest in it, listen to it (for as long as it continues), aware that God is forgiving you, touching your heart and changing you quietly, imperceptibly, into the likeness of his Son.

Action

We can all be judgemental at times, picking out the little 'speck' in our neighbour's eye and ignoring the 'beam' in our own.

Resolve in future to try and radiate to others the love, compassion and understanding that Jesus has just offered you in your communion with him through his word. Be assured that you can do this with the help of his grace.

CHAPTER 2

Praying with Matthew

We now turn to the theme of prayer in Matthew. It is generally agreed that this gospel was written later than Mark. So, it is hardly surprising to find that much of Mark's teaching on prayer reappears in Matthew. This, however, is no mere repetition or expansion of what was already there, in embryo, in the previous gospel. First, then, we need to glance for a moment at the teaching on prayer common to these two evangelists.

A heritage shared[1]

Both Matthew and Mark link prayer with forgiveness. We recall the teaching of Mark: 'Whenever you stand praying, forgive, if you have anything against anyone; so that your Father in heaven may also forgive you your trespasses' (Mk 11:25). These words may well be an early formulation of one of the petitions of the Our Father, for we have that same teaching again right at the heart of the Our Father in Matthew: 'Forgive us our debts, as we also have forgiven our debtors' (Mt 6:12). But just in case we might forget the lesson, Matthew also gives us a kind of appendix to the Lord's Prayer: 'For if you forgive others their trespasses, your heavenly Father will also forgive you; but if you do not forgive others, neither will your Father forgive your trespasses' (Mt 6:14; cf 18:21-35). There is an important link, then, between prayer and forgiveness, one which is common to Matthew and Mark. It is also rightly stressed by at least one great doctor of the church, Teresa of Avila. For her, there is no sign of real progress in prayer – indeed, of prayer in any true sense – without this

---

1. The focus in this section is on the similarities between Matthew and Mark. This does not necessarily exclude points in common with Luke which will be treated in the following chapter.

readiness to forgive. It is, she says, the test of authentic prayer (cf *WP* 36:7-8).

Matthew and Mark also mention the importance of the inner dispositions for prayer. In both gospels, we find a warning against the prayer of the Pharisees and Scribes, which is phrased in almost identical terms: 'You hypocrites! Isaiah prophesied rightly about you when he said: "This people honours me with their lips, but their hearts are far from me"' (Mt 15:7-9; cf Mk 7:6-7; 12:40; Is 29:13). But Matthew is even more emphatic. Again and again, he stresses the importance of these inner dispositions. He does so by contrast with the outward shows, the empty façade of worship. In the Sermon on the Mount, for example, he already warns against the prayer of the 'hypocrites' – which, in the original Greek, literally means 'actors' (Mt 6:5; cf 23:2-8). There is a similar warning in Mark, where it is directed against the prayer of the Scribes who 'for the sake of appearance say long prayers' (Mk 12:40). The language differs somewhat in Matthew, but the lesson is essentially the same: 'Beware of practising your piety before others in order to be seen by them … And whenever you pray, do not be like the hypocrites; for they love to stand and pray in the synagogues and at the street corners, so that they may be seen by others … When you are praying, do not heap up empty phrases' (Mt 6:1, 5, 7). Here already, we come close to the core of Matthew's teaching on prayer. It is about inner dispositions, the secrets of the heart, something known to God alone: 'Go into your room and shut the door and pray to your Father who is in secret; and your Father who sees in secret will reward you' (Mt 6:6). It is an invitation to what we might call, in biblical language, 'truth in the heart' (Ps 50:8).

In Matthew, as in Mark, Jesus withdraws during his ministry in order to pray alone. On two occasions in Mark, Jesus withdraws from the crowd expressly, we are told, to pray (Mk 1:35; 6:46). In Matthew, however, there is only one example of the solitary prayer of Jesus. It occurs, as in Mark (Mk 6:46), between the multiplication of the loaves and Jesus walking towards his disciples on the water. 'He went up the mountain by himself to pray,' writes Matthew (Mt 14:23) – words which will be considered in their context more fully later.

Another point in common between the two evangelists is the lesson on the temple as a house of prayer (Mt 21:12-13; Mk 11:15-17). Both Matthew and Mark link this closely with the episode of Jesus cursing the fig tree (Mt 21:18-19; Mk 11:12-14, 20-21) – a lesson on faith and prayer, and with the promise of an infallible response to the prayer of faith: 'Whatever you ask for in prayer with faith, you will receive' (Mt 21:22; Mk 11:22, 24). Here, as elsewhere, there are in Matthew unmistakable echoes of Mark's teachings on prayer.

Matthew also takes up the warning already found in Mark, to 'beware' and 'keep awake' (Mt 24:4, 42; Mk 13:5, 33); this anticipates a later warning of Jesus which is also linked expressly with prayer in both Matthew and Mark: 'Stay awake and pray' (Mt 26:41; Mk 14:38). In this same context, both these evangelists record similar words: 'Pray that it [Matthew: 'your flight'] may not be in winter' (Mk 13:18; Mt 24:20). Finally, both evangelists give us the example of Jesus himself at prayer in the garden – the Gethsemane prayer (Mt 26:36-46; Mk 14:32-42) – which we will return to at the end of this chapter.

This brief survey, then, highlights the teaching on prayer which Matthew shares with Mark. In all these examples, we can see that the teaching of Matthew was already firmly embedded in Mark. And we can also see how Matthew went beyond that earlier teaching, developing new dimensions about the mystery of prayer.

A heritage complemented
When we read the gospels, however, we cannot help noticing that there are also some passages on prayer in Matthew which he shares with Luke but not with Mark. They provide not only further teachings on prayer, but also new and rich insights into the mystery of Jesus himself at prayer. As we shall see, such passages confirm Mark's insight into the prayer-life of the early Christian community and complement it beautifully.

We find the Lord's Prayer, for example, only in Matthew and Luke. Linked closely with it in both gospels is a precious lesson on persevering prayer a few lines later: 'ask ... search ... knock ...' (Mt 7:7; Lk 11:9). There are obvious similarities, too, between the versions of the Our Father in both gospels. So, there is little doubt that we are here dealing with the same prayer of Jesus. And yet there are also striking differences, revealing how two distinct communities prayed the Our Father and how they treasured, each in their own way, the prayer which Jesus taught them.

Also exclusive to Matthew and Luke is a great prayer of thanksgiving on the lips of Jesus. In it, we penetrate into the mind and heart of Jesus in prayer:

> I thank you, Father, Lord of heaven and earth, because you have hidden these things from the wise and the intelligent and have revealed them to infants; yes, Father, for such was your gracious will. All things have been handed over to me by my Father; and no one knows the Son except the Father, and no one knows the Father except the Son and anyone to whom the Son chooses to reveal him. (Mt 11:25-27; cf Lk 10:21-22)

This prayer is the same, almost word for word, in both gospels. The image is that of a Father in communion with his Son; and a Son, who is receptive, open to his Father's will. This Father-Son relationship in turn finds expression in a complete harmony of wills (cf Jn 10:17-18). In this short but vital passage is revealed the inner mystery of Jesus himself at prayer: a Son in total submission to his Father's will.[2]

Another theme common to Matthew and Luke is the link between prayer and missionary activity; again, this is done in a way which we do not find in Mark. The words are identical in both gospels: 'Therefore ask the Lord of the harvest to send out labourers into his harvest' (Mt 9:38; Lk 10:2). There is no miracle,

---

2. This relationship will be developed at much greater length later, in chap 4 which treats of the priestly prayer in John 17.

no magic formula to extend the kingdom of God. Ultimately, everything depends on the Lord of the harvest and the labourers whom he sends. But we can pray, and know that our prayers will be effective.

All-embracing prayer

We also have common only to Matthew and Luke a lesson in prayer for our enemies, expressed in a very similar way: 'Love your enemies and pray for those who persecute you' (Mt 5:44; Lk 6:27-28); this goes beyond the Old Testament command to love one's own people (Lev 19:18). Here, then, we see how Christian prayer liberates the human spirit. It is also worth noticing the addition in Matthew – the reason which he gives for this lesson on prayer: 'so that you may be children of your Father in heaven' (Mt 5:45). In this way, Matthew brings us much closer to an understanding of Christian prayer as a father-son relationship, like that of Jesus praying to his Father (Mt 11:25-27; 26:39).

But perhaps most striking of all, we have common to Matthew and Luke an important stress on the theme of worship. Both evangelists set their gospels within a framework of worship. In the first chapter of Matthew, we see the Magi coming to 'pay homage' to the child (Mt 2:2) – a phrase which occurs like a refrain in Matthew's description of the scene (Mt 2:2, 8, 11). So, too, Luke's infancy narratives are steeped in an atmosphere of worship and prayer, with everything centred on the temple (Lk 1:8-23; 2:22-38, 41-51). Then, when we look at the conclusion to these two gospels, we find both Matthew and Luke ending in a similar way, with the community worshipping the risen Jesus and additionally, in Luke, blessing God in the temple (Mt 28:9, 17; Lk 24:52-53). We can therefore say that everything in Matthew and Luke is set within a large framework of worship. Each gospel is like an extended record of a vibrant and praying community, providing us with precious insights into the liturgical life of the early church.

A heritage explored

We have so far considered connections between Matthew and the other synoptic gospels. But Matthew also seems to intimate some of the later expansions of the lessons on prayer which we will find in John.

The theme of revelation, so characteristic of John, is central to that prayer of thanksgiving which we have just seen on the lips of Jesus in Matthew and which concludes: 'no one knows the Son except the Father, and no one knows the Father except the Son and anyone to whom the Son chooses to reveal him' (Mt 11:27).[3] Indeed, John's teaching on prayer as an intimate communion between Jesus and his Father in the priestly prayer of the fourth gospel would hardly have been possible without a point of departure like the one which we find in that thanksgiving prayer of Jesus in Matthew – though this does not necessarily mean that John had access to the gospel of Matthew.

There is a further lesson on prayer in Matthew which seems to anticipate John: 'Again, truly I tell you, if two of you agree on earth about anything you ask, it will be done for you by my Father in heaven' (Mt 18:19). Matthew gives the reason why this prayer will be answered: 'For where two or three are gathered in my name, I am there among them' (Mt 18:20). The key words are: 'in my name'. We notice that this teaching on prayer is given to us right at the heart of Matthew's community discourse, with its lesson on fraternal correction (Mt 18:15-18) and forgiveness (Mt 18:21-35). In fact, characteristic of John's gospel is prayer 'in my name' (Jn 14:13-14; 15:16; 16:23-24, 26); and he, too, gives it to us within the framework of his community discourse – at the last supper, with its central lesson on fraternal love (Jn 13:34-35; 15:12-13).

A child at rest

This has necessarily been a brief survey of Matthew's teaching

---

3. This passage is so clearly resonant of the fourth gospel that it has been rightly referred to as 'The Johannine *logion*' ('saying'), and more popularly as 'The Johannine Thunderbolt'.

on prayer in relation to the other gospels. But already we begin to glimpse something of the originality of his teaching. As we have seen, Matthew closely links his insights on prayer with a worshipping community. He also emphasises the inner dispositions for prayer and specifies them further for us when he tells us to pray 'so that you may be children of your Father in heaven' (Mt 5:45). Moreover, he gives us the supreme model of this when he reveals the mind and heart of Jesus himself at prayer – the Son in total submission to his Father's will (Mt 11:25-27; cf 26:36-46).

There is one other original touch in this gospel that is worthy of note. We know that Matthew, Mark and Luke all tell us that children were brought to Jesus (Mt 19:13-15; Mk 10:13-16; Lk 18:15-17). However, Matthew is the only one who tells us that they were brought to him 'in order that he might lay his hands on them and pray' (Mt 19:13). This detail may be easily overlooked, yet it is highly significant for an understanding of prayer in Matthew. Everything in his gospel seems to point to an inseparable link between prayer and the dispositions of a child – a child of God, communing in love with a heavenly Father.

An obedient Israelite

We can now link Matthew's teaching on prayer with the central insight of his gospel and so highlight his own original slant. Earlier, we stressed that each of the evangelists has a central insight, a main concern, and we saw that the main emphasis of Mark is to present Jesus as the Suffering Messiah. Matthew, however, presents Jesus as the obedient Israelite fulfilling God's will as revealed in the old covenant and completed in the new.[4] This is not to say that this perspective occurs in Matthew alone. But it would seem to be Matthew's central insight.

So again and again, we find Matthew telling us that some-

---

4. On the progressive realisation of God's unified plan of salvation which culminates in Christ, see The Pontifical Biblical Commission, *The Jewish People and their Sacred Scriptures in the Christian Bible*, Vatican City: Libreria Editrice Vaticana, 2002, #21, pp 47-50.

thing was done in order that the scriptures might be fulfilled. A prime example of this is the infancy narratives in his gospel (Mt 1-2). There, we have five separate stories all loosely hanging together, and each of them is neatly rounded off by a quotation from the ancient prophets, one of the so-called 'citation-formulas' of Matthew's gospel. We have the announcement to Joseph (Mt 1:18-25); the adoration of the Magi (Mt 2:1-12); the flight into Egypt (Mt 2:13-15); the slaughter of the innocents (Mt 2:16-18); and, finally, the return of the Holy Family from Egypt to settle in Galilee at Nazareth (Mt 2:19-23). Each time, Matthew is at pains to tell us that all these things took place in order that the prophecies might be fulfilled (Mt 1:22; 2:5, 15, 17, 23). As he states later in his gospel: Jesus did not come to abolish the law or the prophets; he came in order that, through his submission to God's will revealed in them, their purpose might be completed and fulfilled in him as the obedient Israelite (cf Mt 5:17-18).

There is another curious feature of Matthew's gospel. He gives us five great discourses. There is the sermon on the mount (Mt 5-7); the missionary discourse (Mt 10); the parable discourse (Mt 13); the community discourse (Mt 18); and, finally, the eschatological discourse (Mt 24-25). Five great discourses. It is likely, as many scholars suggest, that the structure of Matthew's gospel is built around these five large divisions, each one introduced by a brief well-ordered account of the ministry of Jesus. This is the structure which has been accepted by the Jerusalem (and New Jerusalem) Bible, for example, with its headings reflecting this arrangement. The infancy narratives would then serve as a prologue, and the passion-resurrection narratives as an epilogue or climax to the entire gospel. Arranged in this way, Matthew's gospel would certainly be admirably suited to evoke the Pentateuch, the five books of Moses. If that is so, then here again, even in the actual shaping of his gospel, we see the central insight of Matthew at work: Jesus as the fulfilment in person of God's will that is manifested, perfected and fulfilled in him as the obedient Israelite.

Not surprisingly, then, Matthew is at pains to describe the

ideal disciple as the one who does the will of the Father. He distils
the essence of his teaching into a single parable (Mt 21:28-32).
The story has a special importance for Matthew and it is found
only in his gospel. From the outset, it invites a response: 'What
do you think?' Jesus asks (Mt 21:28). A man had two sons, we
are told. He went to one of them and asked him to go and work
in his vineyard that day. At first, the son refused but afterwards
he repented and went. The father then spoke to the other son
and asked him to do the same. This son at first agreed, but afterwards he did not go. Now comes the crucial question from
Jesus: 'Which of the two did the will of his father?' (Mt 21:31).
The answer is obvious: the first. For Matthew, discipleship is
about doing the will of the heavenly Father. So, too, is prayer.
The follower of Jesus is called to be, like the Master, an obedient
Israelite.

A teacher in the community
We saw that for Mark, style is the man. The same is true of
Matthew. His way of writing reflects his main concern. He
avoids the rough style of Mark – the abrupt, even careless, turns
of phrase. Matthew is rather more polished, and sometimes
seems to be correcting Mark. His narrative is well-ordered, with
everything neatly arranged and schematic – a style well suited
to a didactic purpose. Among the evangelists, Matthew is more
obviously a teacher. And notably, the Jesus of Matthew's gospel
is also presented as a teacher (Mt 12:38; 17:24; 19:16; 22:16, 24, 36).
This didactic approach has given its stamp to Matthew's treatment of prayer. We have, in Matthew, more of the teachings, or
sayings, of Jesus on prayer than in any of the other gospels.

Matthew is also regarded as an ecclesial gospel. It is concerned in a special way with the community dimension of the
early church. We can detect in it the unmistakable influence of
the liturgy, the solemn tones of the assembly at worship. We see
this, for example, in Matthew's version of the Our Father: the
petitions are well-balanced and rounded off; they have the
tolling cadences of a liturgical celebration, something which the

petitions of the Lucan version do not have (Mt 6:9-13; cf Lk 11:2-4).

But Matthew has something even more important to tell us about the community. In his gospel, we see that the people of Israel have been led astray by their leaders. So Jesus declares: 'Therefore I tell you, the kingdom of God will be taken away from you and given to a people that produces the fruits of the kingdom' (Mt 21:43). We witness in Matthew the end of the old community and the birth of the new: the new community of the church. So, we must always keep in mind the important community dimension of his teaching on prayer.

Jesus alone at prayer

It is within this general perspective that many of Matthew's dominant themes begin to emerge. Three such leading themes are: the abiding presence of Jesus in the community; a worshipping community; and especially the revelation of Jesus as the Son of God. These are likewise important for an understanding of Matthew's teaching on prayer and occur together, in a particularly striking way, in one central scene of his gospel. This is when Matthew describes how Jesus comes to his disciples walking on the water (Mt 14:24-33). It occurs immediately after we are told that Jesus was alone at prayer (Mt 14:23). Significantly, this is the only time in Matthew that we see Jesus praying alone.

We can picture the scene. Jesus is alone at prayer, up in the hills overlooking the Sea of Galilee. While he is there, the disciples are in difficulty out on the sea. Then comes one of the highpoints of the story, and with it Matthew's revelation of the presence of Jesus with his community. Jesus emerges from his prayer and comes to save them, walking on the water. 'Take heart,' he says to the storm-tossed disciples, 'it is I; do not be afraid' (Mt 14:27). We had that same lesson of his presence at the outset of the gospel, quoting the prophet Isaiah: 'They shall name him Emmanuel', which means, 'God is with us' (Mt 1:23; cf Is 7:14). And it is the same message again with which Matthew ends his gospel, as Jesus gives the promise of his abiding presence: 'I am with you always, to the end of the age' (Mt 28:20).

But Matthew adds another episode to this scene. Jesus beckons Peter to get out of the boat and come to him across the water. There is no parallel to this part of the story in the depiction of this scene in the other gospels (cf Mk 4:35-41; 6:45-52; Lk 8:22-25; Jn 6:16-21). This episode reflects the originality of Matthew but also his concern for the community – the church, which Jesus saves. Indeed, Peter takes on special significance in Matthew's gospel, where he is made the foundation of Christ's church (Mt 16:16-19). So, when Matthew mentions the episode of Peter walking on the water, he is not only heightening the impact of the whole scene but also investing it with an ecclesial dimension. In this light, the saving intervention of Jesus here goes beyond the rescuing of Peter from the waves: it has a special message for the church of Matthew. This episode introduces two further leading themes of the gospel: a manifestation of Jesus' divine identity – already indicated in his words 'it is I', literally: 'I am' (cf Ex 3:14) – and the worshipping community. They fuse together and provide an awesome climax to the story: 'And those in the boat worshipped him, saying, "Truly you are the Son of God"' (Mt 14:33).

This scene, then, has far-reaching relevance for our understanding of the church. Jesus emerges out of his solitary prayer and intervenes to save his struggling followers. He is present at all times in the community, helping the church in its difficulties. He is permanently present there as the Son of God, and as an object of worship. It is surely significant that Matthew will return to the theme of prayer right at the heart of his community discourse (Mt 18:19-20). And there, as we shall see, it is the presence of Jesus that provides the evangelist with the ultimate reason for an infallible response to prayer: 'For where two or three are gathered in my name, I am there among them' (Mt 18:20).

Son of God

At several crucial moments, Matthew returns to that leading theme of his gospel: Jesus as the Son of God. At Caesarea Philippi, we have Peter's profession of faith: 'You are the Messiah' (Mt 16:16). We find it again in Mark (Mk 8:29), with identical words. Yes, Jesus *is* the Messiah. But just notice the addition in Matthew: 'You are the Messiah, the Son of the living God' (Mt 16:16).

In Matthew, the voice at the transfiguration says, 'This is my Son, the Beloved; with him I am well pleased; listen to him!' (Mt 17:5). This is an echo of the heavenly voice at the baptism of Jesus (Mt 3:17; cf Mk 1:11). In Mark's account of the baptism, the voice speaks directly to Jesus: 'You are my Son, the Beloved' (Mk 1:11). In Matthew, it is different however: 'This is my Son, the Beloved' (Mt 3:17). The lesson is for others – this is a gospel that teaches.

Moreover, this emphasis of Matthew on the title 'Son of God' is a constant in his gospel: it occurs throughout the ministry of Jesus and anticipates the account of the passion and death, where it is again emphasised. In Mark, the high priest questions Jesus at the trial: 'Are you the Messiah, the Son of the Blessed One?' (Mk 14:61). But Matthew heightens everything, with both a solemn introduction and the additional title, 'Son of God': 'Then the high priest said to him, "I put you under oath before the living God, tell us if you are the Messiah, the Son of God"' (Mt 26:63).

At the crucifixion itself, we have a scene of mockery. Firstly, it is the passers-by who mock: 'Save yourself, and come down from the cross!' (Mk 15:30). That is how Mark expresses it. But in Matthew it becomes: 'Save yourself! If you are the Son of God, come down from the cross' (Mt 27:40). Then follows the mockery of the chief priests, the Scribes and the elders. In Matthew, they say: 'He trusts in God; let God deliver him now, if he wants to; for he said, "I am God's Son"' (Mt 27:43) – 'God's Son'! We have this same taunt again in Mark but there is no reference whatever to the title 'Son of God' (Mk 15:32).

We notice, too, the climax to the crucifixion in Matthew, which can be contrasted with Mark's account. On the lips of the centurion in Mark, we have the words, 'Truly this man was God's Son!' (Mk 15:39), and he emphasises the humanity of Jesus: 'this man'. But there is no reference to 'this man' in Matthew. He says, literally – and in this order for emphasis – 'Truly, Son of God was this' (Mt 27:54). Here, at the climax of his passion narrative, we have the summit of Matthew's revelation: Jesus is the Son of God.

Sons of a heavenly Father

Jesus is permanently present in the community as the Son of God. But the members of that community are also united with one another as his brothers and sisters. Jesus himself makes the point: 'Call no one your father on earth, for you have one Father' (Mt 23:9). We are all brothers and sisters in the Christian community, all children in the one great family of God.

Moreover, Matthew is eminently concrete and practical. We are brothers and sisters, he explains, only if we do the will of our Father. Again, he is explicit. We recall the scene in his gospel, when we are told that his 'mother and brothers' are standing outside, asking to speak with him. Jesus puts the question: 'Who is my mother, and who are my brothers?' (Mt 12:48). Then he points to his disciples and says: 'Here are my mother and my brothers!' (Mt 12:49). Moreover, he gives the reason: 'For whoever does the will of my Father in heaven is my brother and sister and mother' (Mt 12:50). This is not a slight on Mary, his mother. It is the evangelist's way of emphasising the new bond that must exist within the family of God – the new relationship which finds expression, not in ties of flesh and blood, but in doing God's will as children of the same heavenly Father.

Again and again, Matthew highlights this new spiritual relationship. He does it with special emphasis in the Sermon on the Mount (Mt 5-7), when Jesus speaks of 'my Father … your Father … our Father …' (Mt 7:21; 5:16; 6:9). Here, too, the evangelist affirms what he sees as one of the distinctive marks of a child of

God – doing the will of the Father: 'Our Father ... Your will be done' (Mt 6:9-10). And towards the climax of the sermon, Jesus declares: 'Not everyone who says to me, "Lord, Lord," will enter the kingdom of heaven, but only the one who does the will of my Father in heaven' (Mt 7:21). Almost immediately afterwards, we find the same lesson, expressed in the context of keeping and following Christ's words: 'Everyone then who hears these words of mine and acts on them will be like a wise man who built his house on rock' (Mt 7:24). It is here, right at the heart of the Sermon on the Mount, that we see most clearly the originality of Matthew's teaching on prayer. It is essentially a child of God speaking with its heavenly Father, a member of God's family communing in harmony with its Father's will.

A lesson of great kindness and tender love lies behind Matthew's image of God as Father. A caring shepherd, he searches out the one lost sheep. He leaves the ninety-nine others in the green pastures and goes off among the rocks and the crags to look for the one that has strayed (Mt 18:12-14). Jesus explains: 'So it is not the will of your Father in heaven that one of these little ones should be lost' (Mt 18:14). Matthew's God is a Father who loves and cares for his children, in every detail of their lives. This reflects his special continuity with the Old Testament: the God of the covenant, a God of love and compassion and tenderness (Ex 34:6-7; Ps 102). So when he talks about prayer in his Sermon on the Mount, this is his lesson: 'Therefore I tell you, do not worry about your life, what you will eat or what you will drink, or about your body, what you will wear ... Look at the birds of the air ... Consider the lilies of the field ... your heavenly Father knows that you need all these things' (Mt 6:25-26, 28, 32). In Matthew, God's love is primary.

A catechism of prayer
Matthew gives us the kernel of his teaching on prayer in the Sermon on the Mount. This context has a special significance. No name is given to the mountain. We are not meant to think of any particular mountain. Nor indeed of any particular sermon.

We will find much of Matthew's teaching in this sermon again in Luke, though Luke does not present it as taking place on a mountain (cf Lk 6:17-49). Matthew, however, provides the setting of a mountain in order to evoke Mount Sinai, where God established a covenant relationship with his people. In this way, he is inviting us to consider Jesus' teaching on prayer against this background of the giving of the ten commandments – God teaching his people with the gift of his covenant.

At the heart of the Sermon on the Mount, occupying a large portion of chapter 6, Matthew places a separate, well-ordered and concise section (Mt 6:1-18), with his teaching on prayer at the centre. Here, Jesus speaks first about 'alms' (vv 2-4), then about 'prayer' (vv 5-15), and finally about 'fasting' (vv 16-18). When he speaks of each of these three – almsgiving, prayer and fasting – the evangelist maintains the same pattern or structure. There is a sharp contrast between external observance and inner disposition. When we give alms, when we pray, when we fast, the lesson of Matthew is the same: do not act in order to be seen by others, but do it in secret and so your Father who sees in secret will reward you (cf Mt 6:1).

There is, however, a significant difference when the evangelist speaks of prayer in particular. In this central part (Mt 6:5-15) he begins, as for almsgiving and fasting, with the contrast between external and inner reality: 'And whenever you pray, do not be like the hypocrites; for they love to stand and pray ... so that they may be seen by others ... But whenever you pray ... pray to your Father who is in secret' (Mt 6:5-6). At first, then, it appears that we have the same regular pattern. But Matthew's teaching on prayer does not end there. He breaks the well-ordered pattern by including some additional instructions of Jesus on prayer (Mt 6:7-15).

We do not find this teaching in any of the other gospels – which shows how important it is for Matthew: 'When you are praying,' Jesus says, 'do not heap up empty phrases as the Gentiles do; for they think that they will be heard because of their many words. Do not be like them, for your Father knows what you need before you ask him' (Mt 6:7-8). At this point, Matthew also adds the Our Father (Mt 6:9-13) and a lesson on forgiveness (Mt 6:14-15). It would seem that the evangelist is drawing here on a separate prayer tradition.[5] He first stamps his teaching on prayer with his own special emphasis on the inner dispositions (Mt 6:5-6). But this teaching on prayer, we might say, acts like a magnet, drawing to itself all those additional sayings of Jesus on prayer which were preserved elsewhere in the teaching of the apostles (Mt 6:7-13). This Matthean collection of the sayings of Jesus on prayer is a fine example of an early catechism – a beautiful record of the early church's teaching on prayer – and we shall look at it more closely now. It may well have been used to instruct the newly baptised.

The hidden spring

It will help us to understand Matthew's teaching on prayer if we look at it in the light of its rich implications as the inner room of the heart. Matthew says: 'But whenever you pray, go into your room and shut the door and pray to your Father who is in secret' (Mt 6:6). St Ambrose captures the meaning well:

> You must not think that he means by this a room with four walls separating you physically from others, but the room that is within you, where your thoughts are shut up, the place that contains your feelings. This room of prayer is with you at all times, wherever you go it is a secret place and what happens there is witnessed by God alone.[6]

In the language of Teresa of Avila, this Matthean 'room' becomes an 'interior castle'. Teresa tells her Carmelite sisters that 'the door of entry to this castle is prayer and reflection' (*IC* I:1:7), and she ends her work by urging them to visit it regularly: 'I

---

5. This point is well explained in Jeremias, *op. cit.*, pp 87-9. See especially: 'we have before us the wording for the Prayer from two churches, that is, different liturgical wordings of the Lord's Prayer. Each of the evangelists transmits to us the wording of the Lord's Prayer as it was prayed in his church at that time.' (p 89).
6. Quoted in *Divine Office*, vol III, p 613.

think it will be a consolation for you to delight in this interior
castle since without permission from the prioress you can enter
and take a walk through it at any time' (*IC* Epil. l).

When the evangelist says, 'Go into your room and shut the
door' (Mt 6:6), he is speaking of an inner room in contrast to the
place where the 'hypocrites' love to pray: 'They love to stand
and pray in the synagogues and at the street corners, so that they
may be seen by others' (Mt 6:5). The prayer of the hypocrites is
something external. But, as we well know from Matthew's
gospel, what really matters is the inner disposition – or, in the
biblical sense of the term, the 'heart'.[7] This is the hidden spring
and nerve-centre of a person's whole life and activity. Several
times Matthew speaks about the 'heart' in his Sermon on the
Mount: 'Blessed are the pure in heart'; 'For where your treasure
is, there your heart will be also' (Mt 5:8; 6:21). Even before the
external action ever takes place, it is there in the 'heart' that a
person already commits sin (cf Mt 5:28). However, this 'room' of
Matthew takes on added depth when we consider the 'heart' in
the light of the Old Testament.

A new heart
In the Old Testament, a new covenant was already promised,
and in language that speaks about the 'heart'. As Jeremiah
prophesied: 'I will put my law within them, and I will write it on
their hearts' (Jer 31:33). The contrast there with the covenant on
Sinai is unmistakable. The new law is not written on tablets of
stone – an external law. It is written within – an inner spring.
Ezekiel re-echoes the words of Jeremiah some years later. But he
also clarifies: 'A new heart I will give you, and a new spirit I will
put within you; and I will remove from your body the heart of
stone and give you a heart of flesh. I will put my spirit within
you' (Ezek 36:26-27; cf 11:19-20) – a new law, written within us.
A law of love, a new heart, new spirit. The *Miserere* gives im-

---

7. The *Catechism of the Catholic Church* (#2563) explains well the biblical
sense of heart. See also James McCaffrey, *The Carmelite Charism, op. cit.*,
pp 20-2.

mortal expression in prayer to a longing for this new spirit, this new heart: 'A pure heart create for me, O God, put a steadfast spirit within me' (Ps 50:12).

This promise of a new heart is at last fulfilled with the coming of Jesus. In Paul, the contrast becomes explicit between the law written on tablets of stone and the law written on the human heart. He addresses these words to the Corinthians: 'You show that you are a letter of Christ, prepared by us, written not with ink but with the Spirit of the living God, not on tablets of stone but on tablets of human hearts' (2 Cor 3:3). The same idea recurs, in equivalent language, in Paul's letter to the Romans: 'God's love has been poured into our hearts through the Holy Spirit that has been given to us ... The law of the Spirit of life in Christ Jesus has set you free from the law of sin and of death' (Rom 5:5; 8:2). It is this heart, this love, that Jesus himself asks his Father to give to all believers – to place within them: 'I made your name known to them, and I will make it known, so that the love with which you have loved me may be in them, and I in them' (Jn 17:26). God's eternal love is poured out in our hearts with the gift of the Holy Spirit. This is the inner 'room' of Matthew, already foretold in the Old Testament prophecies. It is this love we release and set free in prayer. This is the new heart that is the perennial spring of all prayer. For that reason, too, Teresa insists: 'the important thing is not to think much but to love much' (IC IV:1:7; cf F 5:2). Not to meditate, in the sense of thinking, but to pray: in an exchange of love, a dialogue with God. It is the Holy Spirit who directs this conversation.

Bombarding God

Matthew goes on to tell us that when we pray we must not 'heap up empty phrases as the Gentiles do; for they think that they will be heard because of their many words' (Mt 6:7). We might consider, for a moment, one kind of prayer described in the First Book of Kings. It gives us some idea of what the evangelist means by heaping up 'empty phrases', or babbling our prayer, and thinking that we will be heard for our many words. This is the prayer of the false prophets of Baal in contest with Elijah on Mount Carmel. They called on the name of their God from morning until noon:

> 'O Baal, answer us!' But there was no voice, and no answer. They limped about the altar that they had made. At noon Elijah mocked them, saying: 'Cry aloud! Surely he is a god; either he is meditating, or he has wandered away, or he is on a journey, or perhaps he is asleep and must be awakened.' Then they cried aloud and, as was their custom, they cut themselves with swords and lances until the blood gushed out over them. As midday passed, they raved on until the time of the offering of the oblation, but there was no voice, no answer, and no response. (1 Kgs 18:26-29)

Bombarding God with 'empty phrases'! This kind of prayer is based on a false concept of God. It feeds on the idea that prayer is a kind of magic formula that can bend God's will to ours by the sheer power of words. It neglects what is essential: prayer is all about bringing our will into harmony with God's will, not his will into harmony with ours. A great teacher of the spiritual life, Teresa of Avila, sums up her entire teaching on prayer in *The Way of Perfection* in these words: 'Everything I have advised you about in this book is directed toward the complete gift of ourselves to the Creator, the surrender of our will to his' (*WP* 32:9; cf *IC* II:1:8). This, ultimately, is Matthew's teaching on prayer.

At one with God's will

In his account of the Sermon on the Mount, Matthew goes on to say: 'Do not be like them.' Here, he is still talking about those who 'heap up empty phrases', the babblers at prayer. 'Do not be like them,' he warns us, 'for your Father knows what you need before you ask him' (Mt 6:8). Then the evangelist gives us his version of the Our Father. It is a well-ordered prayer, a perfect expression and summary of our needs. And it brings us to pray with the whole body of believers who are alive in Jesus. This prayer opens us to the whole world. For we may be alone in the inner 'room'; but when we begin to pray, we enter into the community of all who live and love in Jesus, and we receive their strength in return. The prayer of love transcends all boundaries, even the confines of space and time. God is *our* Father, not just *my* Father.

Moreover, prayer is quite simply a child talking to its heavenly Father, with all the love and intimacy and familiarity that the word 'Father' conveys in Matthew. The Our Father puts first things first – God's honour and glory: 'Hallowed be your name. Your kingdom come. Your will be done' (Mt 6:9-10). Then our needs: a prayer for daily bread, for forgiveness, for protection in temptation, and for deliverance from evil. It is the perfect pattern of all prayer: an address – 'Our Father'; then first things first – God's honour and glory; and finally, everything else secondary to that – our needs.

We should notice in particular the third petition of the Our Father, which we do not find in Luke who has only two petitions that deal directly with God: 'Hallowed be your name. Your kingdom come' (Lk 11:2). In Matthew, however, we have a third: 'Your will be done' (Mt 6:10). This phrase gives a special balance to his prayer – three petitions in the first part concerned directly with God; and three in the second part relating directly to our needs. This balanced shape is an unmistakable sign of the liturgical influence at work in Matthew's gospel and in his teaching on prayer. But it is not just a question of liturgy.

This third petition in Matthew's Our Father contains an extremely important lesson. It in fact gives us a better understanding of the first two petitions common to Matthew and Luke. The words 'Your will be done', special to Matthew alone, are a commentary, as it were, on the meaning of the first two petitions. So, in his version of the Our Father, we see how Matthew's community understood them: God is hallowed – honoured and glorified – and his kingdom comes – his rule, his reign, his saving action – when God's will is done. This takes us right back to the kernel of

Matthew's teaching on prayer. It is a child of God speaking with its heavenly Father and in harmony with his will.

Prayer in the garden
The episode of Gethsemane (Mt 26:36-46) is not only a climax in Matthew's gospel. It also yields up the deepest dimensions of his teaching on prayer, which is perfectly embodied in Jesus at prayer in the garden. A comparison with the account of Mark will further serve to highlight Matthew's original slant. We find in Matthew, for example, a special emphasis on the community aspect of prayer. We recall how Mark introduces the prayer in the garden with these words of Zechariah: 'I will strike the shepherd, and the sheep will be scattered' (Mk 14:27; Zech 13:7). Matthew, however, modifies this quotation from the prophet so that it reads: 'I will strike the shepherd, and the sheep of the flock will be scattered' (Mt 26:31) – not just the sheep, but the sheep of the flock. The community dimension, the ecclesial aspect, comes to the fore once again.

In the garden, Jesus is utterly exhausted and falls on his face. Yet Matthew presents Jesus as still in command of the situation, which is unlike the Jesus of Mark who 'threw himself on the ground and prayed' (Mk 14:35). This action in Mark is repetitive: Jesus stumbles along, falling and rising repeatedly, and praying over and over again. Matthew, however, was writing his gospel mainly for Jewish converts and so, understandably, Jesus takes on the Jewish attitude of prostration in prayer: literally, in the Greek, 'he fell on his face' (Mt 26:39). This posture in prayer, even in his agony, is full of reverence.

But there is another important difference between the Jesus of Mark and the Jesus of Matthew at prayer in Gethsemane. We notice in both gospels that Jesus goes away from his disciples three times, and returns to them again three times. Mark himself does not tell us explicitly that Jesus left his disciples but subtly puts the emphasis on the return of Jesus, which he does mention explicitly on all three occasions (Mk 14:37, 40, 41). In Mark, then, we see a Jesus who, in his agony, experiences a deep need for human companionship and returns to his disciples for support. In Matthew, on the other hand, the emphasis is not on the return of Jesus but on his departure. Matthew tells us that 'he went away' from his disciples three times (Mt 26:39, 42, 44). The focus, then, is not so much on the loneliness of Jesus as on his communion with his Father in prayer.

Perhaps an even more significant lesson for us comes in the content of Jesus' prayer. When he departs from his disciples for a second time, Mark tells us simply: 'And again he went away and prayed, saying the same words' (Mk 14:39). As we have already observed, it is generally taken that Mark's phrase 'the same words' is a reference to the words of Jesus after his first departure: his prayer of surrender to his Father's will (cf Mk 14:36). But they could also be a prayer referring to the words which, in Mark, Jesus has just spoken to his disciples: 'The spirit indeed is willing, but the flesh is weak' (Mk 14:38). If so, then Mark may be heightening again the frailty of the human Jesus and his solidarity with his disciples in their own weakness, as they struggle to stay awake at prayer. Matthew, however, leaves us in no doubt about the content of Jesus' repeated prayer. He tells us explicitly: 'Again he went away for the second time and prayed, "My Father, if this cannot pass unless I drink it, your will be done"' (Mt 26:42). Here, we find the essential mark of prayer in Matthew on the lips of Jesus: 'Your will be done.' It is the third petition of Matthew's Our Father, absent in Luke's version of the prayer.

The human struggle of Jesus in the Gethsemane prayer of Mark does not appear to the same degree in Matthew. We notice that, in Matthew, Jesus seems to be more composed, more serene, more in command of the situation. Mark, emphasising the struggle, is at pains to isolate two distinct stages, as it were, in the prayer of Jesus – his wish for the 'hour' and then for the 'cup' to pass – followed immediately by his surrender to the Father's will: 'And going a little farther, he threw himself on the ground and prayed that, if it were possible, the hour might pass from him. He said, "Abba, Father, for you all things are possible;

remove this cup from me; yet, not what I want, but what you want"' (Mk 14:35-36). Here, we have a direct request that the 'cup' might be removed. It is not so in Matthew. His version of the prayer flows more smoothly in an uninterrupted movement of accepting the Father's will – requesting that the 'cup' be removed from him only if it is possible: 'And going a little farther, he threw himself on the ground and prayed, "My Father, if it is possible, let this cup pass from me; yet not what I want but what you want"' (Mt 26:39).

There is a further difference of emphasis in the two versions of the prayer. Mark stresses the longing of Jesus to be spared the 'hour': 'He threw himself on the ground and prayed that, if it were possible, the hour might pass from him' (Mk 14:35). But the 'hour' is fixed in God's design, determined by God's will. It is surely no coincidence that, in Matthew, Jesus does not pray that the 'hour' will pass from him. He accepts the 'cup' of suffering as part of God's plan. Jesus, in Gethsemane, is the perfect model of prayer for Matthew: total submission to his Father's will, and a giving of himself for his church.

Surrender

As we prepare to leave Matthew, we might ponder on a relevant passage from Teresa of Avila's *Way of Perfection*. Her words, which focus on the prayer of Jesus in the garden, are a profound commentary on Matthew's essential teaching on prayer and its relevance to our own lives:

> 'Your will be done on earth as it is in heaven.' ... Do you want to know how he answers those who say these words to him sincerely? Ask his glorious Son, who said them while praying in the garden. Since they were said with such determination and complete willingness, see if the Father's will wasn't done fully in him through the trials, sorrows, injuries, and persecutions he suffered until his life came to an end through death on a cross ... Unless we give our wills entirely to the Lord so that in everything pertaining to us he might do what conforms with his will, we will never be allowed to

drink from this fount. Drinking from it is perfect contemplation ... (*WP* 32:2, 6, 9)

Teresa's last word on the matter is an exhortation to surrender and sums up Matthew's entire teaching on prayer: 'I give
you one counsel: ... with simplicity and humility, which will
achieve everything, say: *fiat voluntas tua*' (*WP* 32:14).

For Pondering and Prayer

1. Matthew wrote his gospel for converted Jews already familiar with the Old Testament. In what way does this influence his teachings on prayer and the arrangement and style of his gospel?

2. Surrender to God's will is central to Matthew's understanding of discipleship. How is this exemplified in his portrait of Jesus?

3. Matthew closely links his insights on prayer with a worshipping community. In what way does this give his teaching a special importance for a better understanding of prayer?

A GUIDED *LECTIO DIVINA*

The gentle Jesus (Mt 11:25-30)

At that time Jesus said, 'I thank you, Father, Lord of heaven and earth, because you have hidden these things from the wise and the intelligent and have revealed them to infants; yes, Father, for such was your gracious will. All things have been handed over to me by my Father; and no one knows the Son except the Father, and no one knows the Father except the Son and anyone to whom the Son chooses to reveal him. Come to me, all you that are weary and are carrying heavy burdens, and I will give you rest. Take my yoke upon you, and learn from me; for I am gentle and humble in heart, and you will find rest for your souls. For my yoke is easy, and my burden is light.'

Reading

Relax. Invoke the Holy Spirit. Then read this passage slowly, attentively and reverently, with mind and heart open to receive the word, ready to respond to whatever it asks of you. Know that it is a word of love from God addressed to you personally. Reread it two or three times – calmly, quietly and without haste.

Meditation

Take a word or phrase that seems to leap out at you effortlessly from this passage. For example: 'Learn from me; for I am gentle and humble in heart.' This is an advance of love to you from Jesus. Let the words sink slowly into your heart. Consider what they tell you about Jesus ('gentle and humble') and how he teaches ('Come to me … learn from me').

Reflect on the words 'gentle' and 'humble'. Recall someone who has impressed you as gentle and humble. Ponder on what it was in them that appealed to you. Can you remember any other words of Jesus about humility? For example: 'All who humble themselves will be exalted' (Mt 23:12). What is the difference between true and false humility? Think about this with the example of Jesus before your eyes.

Prayer

Jesus extends his invitation of love directly to you: 'Come to me.' Reach out to him with your whole heart. Accept this invitation. Thank him for his gift of 'rest' and his promise to ease your burden of the present moment. You might pray to him like this: 'Jesus, you reveal your secrets to little children. I come to you as your child – weak, needy and defenceless. Draw me deeply into a communion of love with you. Let me rest in you, at peace.'

Contemplation

Jesus is looking at you with a gentle glance of love. Return that glance, keeping the eyes of your heart fixed on him. Be still. No words are needed. Let the silence deepen until it gradually takes over. When your thoughts begin to wander, just ignore them. Hand over your burdens, distractions and anxieties to Jesus. Commune with him quietly, heart to heart. Let yourself be loved.

Action

Recall the words of Jesus: 'You will find rest for your souls.' Resolve in future to try and radiate the serenity, stillness and peace that you have experienced in coming to Jesus and finding 'rest' in his love. It is possible with his help.

CHAPTER 3

Praying with Luke

Prayer is a dominant feature of the gospel of Luke. We have only to consider, for example, the numerous texts which treat explicitly of prayer: the sheer quantity alone far exceeds that in any of the other gospels. But, in a sense, this is hardly surprising. For one thing, Luke repeats much of what Matthew and Mark have to tell us about prayer, so his teaching is firmly embedded in the general gospel tradition on prayer. But Luke also expands on what has been handed on in the tradition.

Not only does Luke have his own original slant on prayer but, more than Matthew even, he seems to intimate in advance some of the later insights developed in John. As we shall see, Luke's originality in his treatment of prayer – as with the other evangelists – is linked with the central insight of his gospel. To try and discover Luke's special approach, it will help if we first look briefly at his teaching on prayer which he has in common with Matthew and Mark; then at what he shares with Matthew alone; and finally – most importantly of all – if we consider the teaching on prayer which we find in Luke independently of these two evangelists.[1]

Solitary prayer of Jesus

As we look at the teaching of Luke on prayer which he shares with Matthew and Mark, we will notice that they all record for us the solitary prayer of Jesus (Lk 5:16; 6:12; 9:18; 11:1; cf Mk 1:35; 6:46; Mt 14:23). But even here, Luke's originality emerges. He highlights this prayer of Jesus in several ways. He includes it

---

1. As John is the last written of the four gospels, we are not concerned here with the relationship between Luke and John: that will be treated later, in the following chapter.

more often, for example, than either Matthew or Mark. And he tells us something else about this solitary prayer of Jesus, which the other evangelists do not tell us – at least not quite as explicitly. On one occasion in the ministry, during a wave of popular enthusiasm and success – apparent success! – we hear the words: 'But now more than ever the word about Jesus spread abroad; many crowds would gather to hear him and to be cured of their diseases' (Lk 5:15). Luke then adds immediately: 'But he would withdraw to deserted places and pray' (Lk 5:16). What the evangelist is saying is that Jesus used to withdraw to the desert places and that he used to pray. This was not just an isolated moment of prayer in a busy and often overcrowded life. Jesus withdrew continually, at regular intervals, from the pressure of his ministry – in search of a quiet place where he could pray alone. It was his custom, and Luke is keen to emphasise this.

In addition, there are episodes common to all three synoptic gospels where Luke alone mentions the prayer of Jesus. Notably, he does this on occasions of great significance. These are generally decisive moments, or turning-points, in the ministry of Jesus. The lesson of Luke is important: there is a need for quiet prayer at all times, but there is a special need at times of heightened significance – the great moments of decision in life. The example of Jesus alone at prayer in Luke is there to confirm it. And this is what we shall consider now.

Prayer and the kingdom

All through his gospel, Luke links prayer with the establishment of the kingdom and the gradual unfolding of the plan of redemption. And he does this in his own original way. We see it especially at the peak moments in the ministry. We find the baptism of Jesus described in all four gospels (Mt 3:13-17; Mk 1:9-11; Lk 3:21-22; Jn 1:29-34). But it is only Luke who tells us that Jesus was at prayer when the Spirit descended. Luke suggests that the Spirit was granted to Jesus here in response to prayer: 'Now when all the people were baptised, and when Jesus also had been baptised and was praying, the heaven was opened, and the

Holy Spirit descended upon him' (Lk 3:21-22). Jesus is launched on his ministry by the power of the Spirit received in prayer.

We are told by the first three evangelists how Jesus chose the Twelve (Mt 10:1-4; Mk 3:13-19; Lk 6:13-15). But it is only Luke who tells us that, before making his choice, Jesus spent the night alone, communing with his Father: 'Now during those days he went out to the mountain to pray; and he spent the night in prayer to God' (Lk 6:12). There is nothing brief, or passing, about this solitary prayer of Jesus in Luke. It lasts deep into the night; it is an extended, protracted prayer. There are two other things of note in this passage. Just before the choice of the Twelve, opposition heightens and the enemies of Jesus become threatening: 'They were filled with fury and discussed with one another what they might do to Jesus' (Lk 6:11). Jesus immediately withdraws to pray, and emerges to choose the nucleus of his future community. Also of note is that only in Luke – the future author of the Acts of the Apostles – are the Twelve explicitly referred to here as 'apostles'. They are men sent to proclaim the kingdom. These Twelve are among 'those who from the beginning were eyewitnesses and servants of the word' (Lk 1:2). The choice of these men has a special significance for Luke, as does the prayer of Jesus with which he emphasises it.

We also find the scene at Caesarea Philippi in the first three gospels (Mt 16:13-20; Mk 8:27-30; Lk 9:18-21). This is a watershed in the ministry of Jesus and marks a peak point in the disciples' experience of him. They now begin to penetrate more deeply into the mystery of his person. But again, it is only Luke who tells us that Jesus on this occasion was at prayer: 'Once when Jesus was praying alone, with only the disciples near him, he asked them, "Who do the crowds say that I am?"' (Lk 9:18).

So, too, the transfiguration is described by the first three evangelists (Mt 17:1-8; Mk 9:2-8; Lk 9:28-36). But it is only Luke who mentions that Jesus went up the mountain to pray, and that it was while he was at prayer that he was transfigured: 'Jesus took with him Peter and John and James, and went up on the mountain to pray. And while he was praying, the appearance of his face changed, and his clothes became dazzling white' (Lk 9:28-29). This link between the prayer of Jesus and his transformation is significant. It is a visible sign of the inner transforming action of God within us at prayer: 'And all of us, with unveiled faces, seeing the glory of the Lord as though reflected in a mirror, are being transformed into the same image from one degree of glory to another; for this comes from the Lord, the Spirit' (2 Cor 3:18).

Dispositions of the heart

Luke stresses the importance of the inner dispositions for prayer. Again, this is something he does in common with Matthew and Mark. Moreover, like the other two evangelists, he brings out a contrast with the prayer of the Scribes and the Pharisees – their pretence, their 'long prayers', and their external observance: 'Beware of the scribes, who like to walk around in long robes, and love to be greeted with respect in the market-places, and to have the best seats in the synagogues and places of honour at banquets. They devour widows' houses and for the sake of appearance say long prayers. They will receive the greater condemnation' (Lk 20:45-47; cf Mk 12:38-40; Mt 23:5-7). These words of Luke are very close to those of Matthew and almost identical to those of Mark; even in the original text, the difference is minimal.

Again in Luke, we find the same lesson of Matthew and Mark on the temple as a 'house of prayer' (Lk 19:46; cf Mk 11:17; Mt 21:13). But Luke, like Matthew, records only these words of Isaiah: 'My house shall be a house of prayer' (Lk 19:46; cf Is 56:7). He does not give us the additional words in Mark: a house of prayer 'for all the nations' (Mk 11:17). This in itself is surprising, for Luke generally stresses the universal dimension of salvation. Moreover, he does not link this teaching with the cursing of the fig tree, as do the other evangelists. Nor does he give us in this same context that great lesson on the link between faith and prayer, with the assurance of an infallible response to the prayer of faith (cf Mk 11:24; Mt 21:22). Elsewhere, however, Luke does stress the link between faith and prayer, in words unique to his gospel. He records the prayer of Jesus for Peter: 'Simon, Simon, listen! Satan has demanded to sift all of you like wheat, but I have prayed for you that your own faith may not fail' (Lk 22:31-32). Jesus builds his church on the faith of Peter, and this in turn rests ultimately on the prayer of Jesus.

Prayer in Luke, as in Matthew and Mark, is a kind of waiting: a patient watching for the God who is still to come, and who *will* come, but in his own time. 'Be alert at all times,' Jesus tells his disciples, 'praying that you may have the strength to escape all these things that will take place, and to stand before the Son of Man' (Lk 21:36). These words of Luke may differ from those of the other evangelists, but the lesson occurs in the same context in all three gospels – the end-perspective of the 'eschatological discourse' – and the teaching itself is essentially the same: watch and pray (Mk 13:18, 33; 14:38; Mt 24:20, 42; 26:41). Finally, we have in these three gospels Jesus himself watching and praying in the Gethsemane scene – the place referred to in Luke as the 'Mount of Olives' (Lk 22:39); this will be considered in some detail at the end of the chapter.

As we have seen, then, many of Luke's teachings on prayer are shared with Matthew and Mark. Like these other two evangelists, he also records the example of Jesus alone at prayer. But even then, Luke gives us his own original slant. Jesus is alone at prayer in Luke more frequently than in any of the other gospels. His solitary prayer is more extended there, too, and reaches far into the night. Luke also stamps the great moments of decision in the life of Jesus as times of quiet, intense prayer.

Reaching out in prayer
In addition to what we have just considered, Luke has important teachings on prayer which he holds in common only with Matthew. We have already referred, in the previous chapter, to the fact that both Luke and Matthew stress the power and necessity of prayer to support the missionary activity of the church. The words are identical in both gospels: 'Ask the Lord of the

harvest to send out labourers into his harvest' (Lk 10:2; Mt 9:38). Prayer in itself is an outreach – apostolic, open, dynamic.

We also have in these two gospels the precept to love and pray for our enemies: 'Love your enemies, do good to those who hate you, bless those who curse you, pray for those who abuse you' (Lk 6:27-28; Mt 5:44). This is a lesson on prayer which is particularly in place in Luke's gospel, with its special universal dimension. It is also a teaching exemplified for us, in his writings, by the prayer of Jesus on the cross: 'Father, forgive them' (Lk 23:34; cf Acts 7:60).

Also common to both Luke and Matthew is that their gospels unfold within a vast liturgical framework. We note in particular that the gospel of Luke begins and ends in the temple, with its worship, prayers and blessings (Lk 1-2; 24:53).

Prayer in the Spirit
We again notice the originality of Luke, when he records some of the actual prayers of Jesus, which he shares only with Matthew. We have the Our Father, for example, in just these two gospels; and closely linked with it in both, the lesson of Jesus on persevering prayer: 'ask ... seek ... knock ...' (Lk 11:5-13; Mt 7:7). Luke illustrates this lesson with a parable which we do not find in Matthew: the story of the troublesome friend who comes at midnight and finally obtains his request (Lk 11:5-8). However, the lesson on perseverance is expressed in almost identical terms in the two gospels. *Almost* identical terms. These are the concluding words of Matthew's version: 'If you then, who are evil, know how to give good gifts to your children, how much more will your Father in heaven give good things to those who ask him!' (Mt 7:11). But we have a subtle variation in Luke: '... how much more will the heavenly Father give the Holy Spirit to those who ask him!' (Lk 11:13). The 'good things' of Matthew become 'the Holy Spirit' in Luke. Luke links prayer, then, explicitly with the Holy Spirit, as he does later in Acts.

We also have common to Luke and Matthew a great prayer of thanksgiving on the lips of Jesus: 'I thank you, Father, Lord of heaven and earth, because you have hidden these things from the wise and the intelligent and have revealed them to infants; yes, Father, for such was your gracious will' (Lk 10:21; Mt 11:25-26).[2] This prayer is identical – almost word for word – in both gospels, even in the original text. The context of the prayer is also virtually the same: rejection of Jesus by the neighbouring towns (Lk 10:13-15; Mt 11:20-24). Jesus is – paradoxically – a Saviour who is rejected and misunderstood. As such, he stands at the centre of God's saving plan and sees this mysterious design of God unfolding: 'such was your gracious will' (Lk 10:21). At this precise moment in both gospels, Jesus bursts into prayer, a prayer of praise and thanksgiving. But again there is a subtle variation in Luke. He introduces the prayer with the words, 'Jesus rejoiced in the Holy Spirit' (Lk 10:21). These words are not in Matthew. So here again, Luke links prayer explicitly with the Holy Spirit.

Prayer parables

Luke also has some important and original teachings on prayer which are not found in any of the other gospels. We have, for example, the two great parables on prayer which are linked together in chapter 18 of Luke, each with its own message. The first is the story of the unjust judge and the woman who comes to him, pleading: the widow whose persevering prayer is finally answered (Lk 18:1-8). Luke had already given us a similar prayer parable about the friend who comes at midnight to beg for bread (Lk 11:5-8) – again, a story found only in Luke. The central message, in both cases, is the same. As the evangelist explains: 'Then Jesus told them a parable about the need to pray always and not to lose heart' (Lk 18:1). This again is Luke's teaching on the necessity of persevering prayer (cf Lk 11:9-13).

The second parable in chapter 18 of Luke is the well-known story of the Pharisee and the tax collector (Lk 18:9-14) – a story

---

2. This Johannine 'logion' is one of the rare and precious insights into how Jesus related to his Father in prayer; another outstanding example is the priestly prayer (Jn 17) which is the subject of chap 4.

unique to Luke. Again, the evangelist explains the central message: 'He also told this parable to some who trusted in themselves that they were righteous and regarded others with contempt' (Lk 18:9). This is a telling lesson on prayer, and the story which illustrates it is beautifully told. After the self-righteousness of the Pharisee, we have the humble attitude of the tax collector: 'But the tax collector, standing far off, would not even look up to heaven, but was beating his breast and saying, "God, be merciful to me, a sinner!"' (Lk 18:13). So simple! It is a prayer of perfect trust and confidence in God; it is an example, too, of our utter poverty and helplessness at prayer, and of our need of God's mercy.

In these two parables, then, we touch on an important aspect of the originality of Luke's teaching on prayer. For him, it is a matter of perseverance, like the prayer of the widow who pleads incessantly. It is also an exercise in humility, like the prayer of the tax-collector, the public sinner. We come to pray with empty hands, fragile and vulnerable, weak and sinful – in need. We lay bare our spiritual poverty in prayer and place our trust in the infinite mercy of God.

Luke will exemplify this prayer of trust later in his gospel, with the cry of Jesus himself on the cross. We find two prayers on the lips of the dying Jesus in Luke's gospel, and we find them only in Luke: the prayer of Jesus for his enemies, 'Father, forgive them; for they do not know what they are doing' (Lk 23:34; cf Acts 7:60); and a prayer of confidence and trust, 'Father, into your hands I commend my spirit' (Lk 23:46; cf Acts 7:59). They both confirm important aspects of Luke's teaching on prayer.

We have also in this gospel – and again only in Luke – the episode of Martha and Mary (Lk 10:38-42). We find it just after the story of the Good Samaritan (Lk 10:30-37) and before Jesus teaches the Our Father (Lk 11:1-4). Its message is clear – prayer is a listening to the word of God: 'There is need of only one thing. Mary has chosen the better part, which will not be taken away from her' (Lk 10:42). Moreover, it is a 'listening' in the true biblical sense of the term – listening and responding, like Mary, the mother of Jesus, surrendering with her *fiat*: 'Let it be with me according to your word' (Lk 1:38).[3]

Even this brief survey of Luke's general teaching on prayer already reveals the genius of Luke and the originality of his insights. In a word, prayer in Luke is closely linked with the Holy Spirit and with the establishment of the kingdom. It is a humble, persevering, trusting prayer; and it is a listening to the word of God.

A vision of salvation history

All this rich teaching on prayer fits easily into place within Luke's vision of salvation history. Luke, as mentioned, wrote not just his gospel but also the Acts of the Apostles. They are, in fact, two complementary volumes of one great work, together showing the full range of Luke's vision. Among the evangelists, Luke is the historian. He reveals the historian's concern in so many ways. He likes to give an explanation of how events unfold in a concrete historical sequence. The ascension, for example, is mentioned in two gospels other than Luke's (Mk 16:19; Jn 20:17), but it is only Luke who gives us a description of it (Lk 24:50-52; Acts 1:9-11). In his gospel, he gives the impression that it took place shortly after the resurrection. In Acts, though, he is more specific: he places it forty days later and so gives it a precise historical sequence (Acts 1:3). The ascension has a special importance for Luke: it marks the end of the ministry and life of Jesus, and the beginning of the time of the church.

Moreover, Luke is not just a writer of ordinary history. He is a writer of salvation history – a sequence of events which is guided by the hand of God, history with a divine purpose. This history Luke divides into three great periods: the time of the prophets (up to and including John the Baptist); the time of Jesus, the great central period often known as 'the middle of time' (his ministry culminating in the ascension); and the time of the church (beginning at Pentecost with the gift of the Spirit, and reaching until the end of time).

---

3. For a discussion of Mary as a model of prayer in the gospels, see James McCaffrey, *The Carmelite Charism, op. cit.*, pp 103-23.

This may seem to us a very simple division: the period of the promises; the period of Jesus' earthly sojourn; and the period of the church, or of the Holy Spirit. But this division of history was, in fact, a great discovery of Luke. He and his community were faced with the problem of the second coming. The early church believed that, with the death of Jesus, the end had already come (cf Mt 10:23; Mk 9:1; 13:30). But when Luke wrote his gospel and Acts, there had already been half a century of church history and still Jesus had not yet returned. Luke solved that problem with his third period of salvation history, or what we call the age of the church: the time of the Spirit, the time of waiting. Luke had a broad and unified vision of salvation history ending with the *parousia*, the second coming.

Centred in Jerusalem

We can easily see how Luke arranges his gospel and Acts around his vision of salvation history. His gospel begins in Jerusalem (Lk 1-2). Then, at the heart of it, there is a long journey of Jesus (Lk 9:51-19:44). It occupies over one third of the gospel. Right from the start of the journey, the evangelist directs our attention towards Jerusalem and even to the ascension of Jesus: 'When the days drew near for him to be taken up, he set his face to go to Jerusalem' (Lk 9:51). The movement of his gospel hurries forward to Jerusalem. Luke reminds us repeatedly that Jesus is on a journey (Lk 9:51, 57; 10:38; 13:22), with Jerusalem as his goal (Lk 9:51; 13:33; 17:11). He alone of the evangelists centres all the apparitions of the risen Jesus in Jerusalem (Lk 24; cf Mt 28:10; Mk 16:7; Jn 21:1-14). And it is in Jerusalem, too, that the gospel ends, with the ascension of Jesus: 'He withdrew from them and was carried up into heaven' (Lk 24:51). Luke will describe the ascension again in similar terms at the beginning of Acts: Jesus was 'lifted up' and 'has been taken up' (Acts 1:9.11). And so the life and ministry of Jesus, the second period of salvation history, comes to an end.

But Luke also leaves us in suspense at the end of his gospel, waiting with the disciples: 'And see, I am sending upon you what my Father promised; so stay here in the city until you have been clothed with power from on high' (Lk 24:49). Acts takes up again the events of the gospel. Here, the ascension is again described (Acts 1:9-11). But we are still waiting in suspense, as we see from the words spoken by Jesus just before his ascension: 'You will receive power when the Holy Spirit has come upon you; and you will be my witnesses in Jerusalem, in all Judea and Samaria, and to the ends of the earth' (Acts 1:8). Then the Spirit descends at Pentecost, ushering in the third period of salvation history: the church is launched on its prophetic mission in the power of the Spirit as a witness to proclaim the good news to the world (Acts 2:1-4). The unfolding of this mission is the story of Acts. No wonder it has sometimes been called the gospel of the Holy Spirit. Everything that happens in the gospel – the time of the life and ministry of Jesus, or 'the middle of time' – is made present again in the time of the church, through the working of the Spirit.

All this helps us to grasp the central insight of Luke's gospel: Jesus is the Spirit-filled prophet. And as we see from Acts, the church itself is this same Spirit-filled prophet: Christ now spread out in the world until the end of time. But if Jesus is the Spirit-filled prophet in the gospel, he is so because he has listened to the word in his prolonged periods of silent prayer – on the mountains, in desert places, and deep into the night. Luke calls every believer to be a Spirit-filled prophet like Jesus. This is only possible for the disciple who has first 'sat at the Lord's feet and listened to what he was saying' (Lk 10:39). It is hardly surprising, then, if we find Luke's original angle on prayer in the gospel repeated again in Acts. Even a cursory glance at the praying church there will confirm this for us.

A praying church

The heart of the church is revealed in Acts. It is a praying church, waiting for the Spirit, with the mother of Jesus in the midst of the community of believers: 'All these were constantly devoting themselves to prayer, together with certain women, including

Mary the mother of Jesus, as well as his brothers' (Acts 1:14). The early church is also a listening church: 'They devoted themselves to the apostles' teaching and fellowship, to the breaking of bread and the prayers' (Acts 2:42). At the same time, it is a praising church: 'Day by day, as they spent much time together in the temple, they broke bread at home and ate their food with glad and generous hearts, praising God' (Acts 2:46-47).

An unending stream of prayer ascends to God in Acts. This is the persevering prayer of Luke's gospel. One such scene has been called 'The Little Pentecost': 'When they had prayed, the place in which they were gathered together was shaken; and they were all filled with the Holy Spirit and spoke the word of God with boldness' (Acts 4:31). When Peter is thrown into prison, we are told that 'the church prayed fervently to God for him' (Acts 12:5). He escapes and returns to the house of his friends 'where many had gathered and were praying' (Acts 12:12). Paul and Silas in prison, too, 'were praying and singing hymns to God' (Acts 16:25). Peter and John pray over the people of Samaria (Acts 8:14-17). All through Acts the church grows and expands under the powerful action of the Holy Spirit: 'Meanwhile the church throughout Judea, Galilee, and Samaria had peace and was built up. Living in the fear of the Lord and in the comfort of the Holy Spirit, it increased in numbers' (Acts 9:31).

In this way, the plan of salvation gradually unfolds in Acts. God's kingdom comes. Just as in Luke's gospel, where Jesus prays with particular intensity at turning-points in his ministry, so in Acts we find the church in prayer at all the peak moments, open to the Spirit. This was especially so at Pentecost (Acts 1:14; 2:1-4) but not only then. There is the episode where Cornelius, the pagan centurion, and his household are converted. It is a crucial moment. We are told that Peter was at prayer when the messengers came to him from Cornelius (Acts 10:9; cf 10:30-31). We are also informed that Cornelius himself 'was a devout man who feared God with all his household ... and prayed constantly to God' (Acts 10:2). In the description of the conversion itself, we find again those essential ingredients of prayer in Luke's gospel: the action of the Holy Spirit, and a listening to the word of God. We read: 'The Holy Spirit fell upon all who heard the word. The circumcised believers who had come with Peter were astounded that the gift of the Holy Spirit had been poured out even on the Gentiles' (Acts 10:44-45).

The first deacons are chosen in Acts so that the apostles might devote themselves more fully 'to prayer and to serving the word' (Acts 6:4). This was a crucial decision in the early church. But Luke's description of the death of the deacon Stephen, the first Christian martyr, also highlights the power of prayer: 'While they were stoning Stephen, he prayed' (Acts 7:59). So, too, Luke subtly links this prayer of the first Christian martyr with the later conversion of Paul: 'The witnesses,' he tells us, 'laid their coats at the feet of a young man named Saul' (Acts 7:58). As one early writer has expressed it: '[Stephen's] holy and untiring love ardently desired to acquire as converts by his prayers those whom he had been unable to convert by argument. And now Paul rejoices with Stephen'.[4] In this prayer of Stephen, Luke re-echoes the prayer of Jesus himself for his enemies: 'Father, forgive them …' (Lk 23:34). And this again exemplifies the lesson of his gospel: 'Love your enemies … pray for those who abuse you' (Lk 6:27-28). But at this point in Acts, Luke also seems to affirm the place and efficacy of prayer in the missionary activity of the church.

Paul – a man of prayer[5]

Luke was writing here in anticipation of the conversion of Paul. This is a great turning-point in the story of Acts. In fact, Luke describes it for us three times (Acts 9:1-9; 22:6-11; 26:12-18). Paul is surely one of the most interesting figures in the history of the

---

4. St Fulgentius of Ruspe, in *Divine Office*, vol I, p 49*.
5. On Paul as a man of prayer, see James McCaffrey OCD, *A Biblical Prayer Journey in the Holy Land* [co-authored], Burgos: Editorial Monte Carmelo, 1998, Appendix IV: Jean Lévêque, 'Pastoral Prayer of St Paul', pp 538-70.

church: Saul, the unconverted, riding around the sea of Galilee, but soon to carry the message, preached along that same lakeside, to the countries washed by the Mediterranean sea. But we notice, here again, Luke's stress on prayer in the story of Paul's conversion – and, as in the gospel, the linking of prayer with the Holy Spirit (cf Lk 10:21; 11:13): we are told that Paul would be 'filled with the Holy Spirit' (Acts 9:17) as God's 'instrument' (Acts 9:15). Immediately after his conversion, Luke records: 'At this moment he [was] praying' (Acts 9:11). Paul then returns to Jerusalem and we are told that he was 'praying in the temple' (Acts 22:17). There he heard the words of the risen Jesus: 'Go, for I will send you far away to the Gentiles' (Acts 22:21). But Paul's sin is always before him, his mind filled with the thought of Stephen, even as he prays: 'And while the blood of your witness Stephen was shed,' Paul says to the Lord, 'I myself was standing by, approving and keeping the coats of those who killed him' (Acts 22:20). Once again, we notice Luke's stress on the link between the death of Stephen and the mission of Paul to the Gentiles – again a subtle hint, it would appear, of the power of Stephen's prayer for the spread of the kingdom.

As Luke tells us, Paul set out on his first missionary journey in the power of the Holy Spirit at work in the praying church: 'While they were worshipping the Lord and fasting, the Holy Spirit said, "Set apart for me Barnabas and Saul for the work to which I have called them." Then after fasting and praying they laid their hands on them and sent them off' (Acts 13:2-3). Finally, at the end of Acts, Paul stands in Rome – a witness to the gospel at the centre of the then-known world.

This is just a rapid survey of Acts. It is necessarily selective. But we can see clearly that the originality of Luke's teaching on prayer, as seen in his gospel, reveals itself again in action when he describes the early church at prayer. There in Acts, as in Luke's gospel, prayer is closely linked with the Holy Spirit and with the establishment of the kingdom. It is a persevering, trusting prayer. It is a listening to the word of God.

The ascending movement of prayer

We return now to Luke's teaching on prayer in the gospel. Much of it is given within the framework of the journey of Jesus to Jerusalem, to his passion and resurrection (Lk 9:51-19:44). This arrangement might be compared to Matthew's Sermon on the Mount (Mt 5-7), in that the journey of Jesus provides Luke with an ideal framework for his teaching on prayer. In this context, prayer itself can easily be seen as a kind of journey along the path traced out by Jesus himself when he travelled to his passion and resurrection. Perhaps nowhere else in his gospel does Luke highlight more effectively for us this important aspect of his teaching on prayer: a journey into the heart of the paschal mystery.

At the outset of the journey, the evangelist describes the passion and resurrection for us in a rather strange way. He uses the Greek word *analêmpsis* which means literally 'a taking up': 'When the days drew near for him to be taken up, he set his face to go to Jerusalem' (Lk 9:51). The assumption of Elijah into heaven (2 Kgs 2:11) provides an Old Testament background for Luke's use of the term. This journey of Jesus, though, is not just a physical movement in space but has a deeper spiritual import. It embraces the passion-resurrection-ascension of Jesus – a whole sequence of events – in one single heaven-directed movement of ascent.

But the ascension of Jesus in Jerusalem, as we have seen, also marks a significant moment in Luke's broad vision of salvation history. It is the climax to the earthly life of Jesus and marks the end of his ministry, that second period of salvation history or 'the middle of time'. It is also a great turning-point for Luke in the future establishment of the kingdom of God. We notice in particular that the evangelist designedly punctuates the journey of Jesus to Jerusalem with repeated references to prayer (Lk 10:2, 21-22, 38-42; 11:1-13; 18:1-8, 9-14). In this way, we discover the importance of prayer for Luke in God's universal plan of salvation. But we also see that prayer is linked in an intimate way with the whole ascending movement of Jesus to heaven through

his passion-resurrection. This kind of spiritual ascent to God by
dying and rising is the inner reality of all true Christian prayer.

Listening to God

It is within the context of the journey of Jesus to Jerusalem that we
find the story of Martha and Mary (Lk 10:38-42). As mentioned,
this episode occurs only in Luke's gospel. Hence, its special importance for an understanding of his teaching on prayer. The
central message about prayer is clear and simple: it is a listening
to the word of God. We will consider the full impact of this scene
presently in the light of the immediate context.

Luke introduces the story by saying: 'Now as they went on
their way ...' (Lk 10:38). Jesus, we recall, is on his journey: 'He
entered a certain village, where a woman named Martha welcomed him into her home. She had a sister named Mary, who sat
at the Lord's feet and listened to what he was saying' (Lk 10:38-
39). That is her prayer: listening to the word of God. The story
continues: 'But Martha was distracted by her many tasks; so she
came to him and asked, "Lord, do you not care that my sister has
left me to do all the work by myself? Tell her then to help me"'
(Lk 10:40). We used to get great mileage out of this story in the
past, to prove the superiority of the contemplative over the active life. But nothing could be farther from Luke's mind. There is
not a word of condemnation by Jesus of Martha's activity. She is
doing a very useful service, a necessary one. As Teresa of Avila
once said: 'The Lord walks among the pots and pans' (*F* 5:8).
There is no reprimand to Martha whatever for her service, no
suggestion that it is unimportant or useless.

But the words of Jesus to Martha contain a very important
lesson for us just the same. She was 'distracted' with much service (Lk 10:40). So, Jesus says to her, 'Martha, Martha, you are
worried and distracted by many things; there is need of only one
thing. Mary has chosen the better part, which will not be taken
away from her' (Lk 10:41-42). She is 'worried' in a way that Luke
warns us about later in his gospel: 'Therefore I tell you, do not
worry about your life, what you will eat, or about your body,

what you will wear … Instead, strive for his kingdom, and these things will be given to you as well' (Lk 12:22, 31; cf Mt 6:25, 33). Martha is worried, so her attention is divided. Her priorities are wrong: she is troubled, anxious, without a centre (cf Jn 14:1).

We can also see why Luke places this episode of Martha and Mary immediately after his teaching on love – love of God and love of neighbour – stressing the intimate and inseparable link between the two aspects of true love: 'You shall love the Lord your God with all your heart, and with all your soul, and with all your strength, and with all your mind; and your neighbour as yourself' (Lk 10:27; cf Deut 6:5; Lev 19:18). Luke will even high-light the importance of service to others in this same context with his story of the Good Samaritan (Lk 10:30-37), another episode to be found only in Luke. It is a beautiful lesson in prac-tical Christianity: 'Go and do likewise' (Lk 10:37). These final words of the parable immediately precede the episode of Martha and Mary, which is a story about priorities in the exercise of love, an appeal for the 'undivided' heart, a total commitment of ourselves to put God at the centre of our lives. First things first, and then everything else falls into place.

This story of Martha and Mary would seem to have a special relevance for our postmodern age. We are indeed an 'anxious' people, a 'worrying' breed, occupied and preoccupied about so many things, like Martha. We forget that ultimately 'there is need of only one thing' (Lk 10:42). We fail to put God at the cen-tre of our lives. Yet for all our stress and striving, we are left with the deep malaise of life today, that most human of all human suffering: loneliness. The lesson of Martha and Mary challenges us to shift the point of gravity to a still-point at the centre of our lives, to move from the 'many things' to the 'one thing' that is the priority. It is also a call to the prayer of recollection or cent-ring prayer, in which we focus on the presence of God in the centre of our soul. There, in that quiet shrine, we too can listen in silence to the word of God – like Mary of Bethany at the feet of Jesus.

A model of perfect prayer

Immediately after the story of Martha and Mary, Luke introduces the Our Father as Jesus continues on his journey. This is a prayer that puts our priorities in their right order. God first: a prayer that he may be hallowed and his kingdom come (Lk 11:2). Then petitions for our needs: a prayer for daily bread, forgiveness, and help in time of trial (Lk 11:3-4). Jesus is telling us *what* we ought to ask for in prayer and *how* we should pray to the Father, at one with the community of believers in the Spirit. Tertullian calls the Our Father a 'summary of the whole gospel' in prayer-form.[6] The Our Father also induces the proper dispositions: the attitude of a child. As in Matthew, the wording of the Our Father in Luke is a salutary reminder that God is the primary agent at work in prayer. That is the import of the words: 'Hallowed be your name. Your kingdom come' (Lk 11:2). Our efforts are not excluded. But it is the Father's action that is primary. We merely cooperate.

In the opening verse (Lk 11:1), Luke describes several of the circumstances in which Jesus taught his disciples how to pray. Each detail is highly significant: 'He was praying in a certain place, and after he had finished, one of his disciples said to him, "Lord, teach us to pray, as John taught his disciples"' (Lk 11:1). Jesus was praying, then, in a certain place. But what place? We are not told. This could have been any place. Indeed, that is what the evangelist seems to suggest. It is just another of those many places referred to in the gospel, where Jesus, we are told, went off alone to pray, to commune with his Father (cf Lk 5:16).

The evangelist, we have seen, also tells us that 'one of his disciples said to [Jesus], "Lord, teach us to pray"' (Lk 11:1). One of the disciples! Which of them? We are not told. It could be any disciple. It could be you and it could be me. In fact, that is the lesson intended by Luke. He is purposely vague and indefinite, as he so often is throughout this journey to Jerusalem, when referring to people or places (cf Lk 9:52, 57-62; 10:38). In this way, the evangelist opens up a universal perspective and speaks to a

---

6. Tertullian, *De Oratione* 1; cf *Catechism of the Catholic Church* #2761.

wider audience, broadening the relevance of his lesson. It is
every disciple and follower who now asks Jesus for a lesson in
prayer. The whole community of his disciples listens to the
word of God as Jesus answers, 'When you pray, say: Father' (Lk
11:2).

Indeed, the Our Father in Luke is a beautiful example of listening to the word of God and also of contemplating Jesus. The
disciples see Jesus once again alone at prayer. They want to pray
like him. So, they say to him: 'Teach us to pray' (Lk 11:1) – meaning: in the way we have just seen you at prayer. Whenever I read
that verse in Luke, I remember something once said by Thérèse
of Lisieux. She tells us that, as a child, in order to know how to
pray she had only to look at the face of her own father absorbed
in prayer.[7] For John Paul II, too, the example of his father at
prayer had a decisive influence on his early years, and he later
said: 'Sometimes I would wake up during the night and find my
father on his knees, just as I would always see him kneeling in
the parish church. We never spoke about a vocation to the
priesthood, but *his example was in a way my first seminary*, a kind
of domestic seminary.'[8] I feel that is the lesson of Luke here too.
We wish to pray. So Luke is saying to us: look at the face of Jesus
himself absorbed in prayer. His example is contagious.

The prayer of the church
The disciples ask Jesus to teach them to pray 'as John taught his
disciples' (Lk 11:1). Why the addition? Earlier in his gospel,
Luke had written: 'John's disciples, like the disciples of the
Pharisees, frequently fast and pray' (Lk 5:33); this phrase has a
parallel in two of the other gospels as well (Mt 9:14; Mk 2:18).
But only Luke speaks of prayer in this connection. John's disci-
ples had their own special form of prayer, and so had the
Pharisees. So, too, had the Essene community at Qumran. A cer-

---

7. See *Story of a Soul: The Autobiography of Saint Thérèse of Lisieux*,
Washington, DC: ICS Publications, 1996, p 43.
8. John Paul II, *Gift and Mystery: On the Fiftieth Anniversary of My Priestly
Ordination*, London: Doubleday & Catholic Truth Society, 1997, p 20.

tain kind of prayer was the distinctive mark of these religious groups. Their prayer marked them off as members of a distinct community. That is what the disciples are asking for: a prayer that would stamp them as the disciples of Jesus. The Our Father is the prayer of the new community of Jesus: the church.

The Our Father is indeed the prayer of the church. In the early days, it was only after the catechumens had been baptised, having been made completely one with Jesus, that they were permitted to say this prayer.[9] We must remember, too, that the disciples of Jesus already knew how to pray. Their minds were steeped in the Old Testament – the psalms, for example, that incomparable prayer-book of Jesus himself. But they still felt the need for something new. They wanted a new kind of prayer. So Jesus gave them the Our Father: a new prayer. That is what Christian prayer is: a new reality. It is like the church itself, and like every baptised follower of Jesus: 'a new creation' (2 Cor 5:17).

We also recall that the disciples waited until Jesus had ceased praying before they asked him to teach them to pray: 'After he had finished, one of his disciples said to him, "Lord, teach us to pray"' (Lk 11:1). Why did they wait for him to end his prayer? Is there not perhaps a hint here of the mystery which surrounded Jesus himself at prayer? How his attitude of reverence and awe must have shimmered through! We like to speak of Jesus as a man for others, the model of Christian action, one uncompromisingly available to all. Indeed, so he is. But we must never forget that, above and before all else, Jesus belongs to the Father. He is, first and foremost, the Adorer. It is only because of his prayer that he can be a man for others. Jesus was open to all people because he was transparent to his Father. Without the silent prayer – the hidden years, the desert, the listening, the inner

9. See Jeremias, *op. cit.*, pp 82-3: 'The position in the Service where the Lord's Prayer was prayed is to be noted: it came immediately before the Communion. As a constituent part of the Communion liturgy, the Lord's Prayer belonged to that portion of the Service in which only those who were baptised were permitted to participate, i.e., it belonged to the so-called *missa fidelium* or "Service for the baptized".'

room and the lonely garden – there could be no compassion for
the needy, no love for the loveless, no healing for the sick.

It is said that there is a crisis of prayer today. Perhaps this is
so. But the crisis seems to be deeper than prayer itself. It affects
our very sense of God, the reality of his transcendent being. The
first requisite for prayer is this sense of God, the holiness of God.
Worship itself means 'worth-ship'. It is our confession of what
God is worth, our avowal that he alone is worthy of praise, adoration, service and thanks. In a word, it is our 'yes' to the fact that
God is God. We praise him for his glory. The disciples must
have seen it all reflected there in the face of Jesus absorbed in
prayer, in his awe, in his reverence. They waited until he
'ceased' praying. They would not dare to interrupt him.

The coming of the kingdom

It is within the context of this same journey of Jesus to Jerusalem
that Luke gives us his great lesson on persevering prayer: 'ask …
seek … knock …' (Lk 11:5-13; cf Mt 7:7-11). Here, he mentions
the Holy Spirit explicitly as God's response to our prayer of
searching: 'How much more will the heavenly Father give the
Holy Spirit to those who ask him!' (Lk 11:13). Some of the fathers
of the church have a very significant variant reading in Luke for
the familiar petition of the Our Father, 'Your kingdom come' (Lk
11:2). Theirs is almost certainly not the original text, but it gives
a marvellous insight into the mind of Luke, when he speaks of
the kingdom and refers to the Holy Spirit as the response to persevering prayer. Instead of the words, 'Your kingdom come', we
find the reading, 'Thy Holy Spirit come upon us and cleanse
us.'[10] This replacement of the 'kingdom' by the 'Holy Spirit' is
perfectly in line with Luke's broad vision of salvation history. At
the beginning of Acts, the disciples ask the risen Jesus about the
kingdom: 'Lord, is this the time when you will restore the kingdom to Israel?' (Acts 1:6). And Jesus replies by promising the
coming of the Spirit: 'You will receive power when the Holy

10. The Fathers in question are Gregory of Nyssa (d 394) and Maximus
Confessor (d 662), as quoted in Jeremias, *op. cit.*, p 83.

Spirit has come upon you' (Acts 1:8). It is through the action of
the Spirit, in response to persevering prayer, that the kingdom
comes and is gradually realised in the church until the end of
time.

Already in Luke, then, we have intimations of the later developments which will take place throughout the period of the
church. Taking the Our Father again, we find that both in
Matthew and in Luke, we read the same petition for daily bread.
But there is a noticeable difference. Matthew's version reads:
'Give us this day (*sêmeron*) our daily bread' (Mt 6:11) – an urgent
prayer for bread for today; while Luke's version reads: 'Give us
each day (*kath' hêmeran*) our daily bread' (Lk 11:3) – a prayer for
God to keep on giving it to us every day. This is an important
shift of perspective. For Luke understands the petition in terms
of our daily needs, like the manna in the desert: 'I am going to
rain bread from heaven for you, and each day the people shall
go out and gather enough for that day' (Ex 16:4). For Luke, this
petition of the Our Father is being fulfilled continually, here and
now, throughout the course of history. We speak of eschatology,
or the 'last things', taking place in the church continually, here
and now, through the working of the Spirit in anticipation of the
end of time. This illustrates perfectly the perspective of Luke.

God's gift of himself

Jesus' reference to the gift of the Holy Spirit, when we 'ask',
'seek' or 'knock' (Lk 11:9-13), also gives us a solution to the great
problem of prayer that is – apparently – unanswered. The gospel
is here telling us that prayer is always answered. Luke is even
explicit about this later in his gospel: 'If you had faith the size of
a mustard seed, you could say to this mulberry tree, "Be uprooted
and planted in the sea," and it would obey you' (Lk 17:6). Other
evangelists repeat the same lesson (cf Mt 17:20; 18:19; 21:21-22;
Mk 11:23-24). So prayer, we are told, always receives an infallible
response. Yet that does not seem to be our experience. So many
things we ask for, and so many things we do not receive. Just listen
again to what Luke says: 'How much more will the heavenly

Father give the Holy Spirit to those who ask him!' (Lk 11:13). That is the unfailing response to every prayer: the gift of the Holy Spirit. Perhaps no one has given us a more perfect comment on Luke's teaching about God's gift of himself in response to persevering prayer than Mother Teresa of Calcutta. One day, Malcolm Muggeridge asked her what she thought about prayer. This was her reply: 'Prayer,' she said, 'enlarges the heart until it is capable of containing God's gift of himself. Ask and seek, and your heart will grow big enough to receive him and keep him as your own.'[11]

Perhaps that is why Paul says to the Corinthians, 'Our heart is wide open' and exhorts them: 'Open wide your hearts also' (2 Cor 6:11, 13). It is a message passed on by many of the saints. Augustine, for example: '[God] wants our desire to be exercised in prayer, thus enabling us to grasp what he is preparing to give. That is something very great indeed; but we are small and limited vessels for the receiving of it. So we are told: "Widen your hearts".'[12] This is the lesson, too, of the Curé of Ars: 'My children, your hearts are small, but prayer enlarges them and renders them capable of loving God.'[13] John of the Cross captures the idea beautifully in a line of perhaps his greatest poem, 'The Living Flame': 'how tenderly you swell my heart with love' (*LF*, stanza 4). When Teresa of Avila wanted to explain the effect of prayer, she borrowed a phrase from the psalms: '*dilatasti cor meum*', meaning 'you have expanded my heart' (Ps 118:32; cf *IC* IV:1:5). You have increased my capacity for yourself!

We receive God when we pray. He works a gradual transformation in our lives. He is living in us, active and dynamic – healing, teaching, guiding, renewing. Prayer is first and foremost this active presence of the Holy Spirit in our hearts. We respond to the transforming power of his love as we remain open, receptive and docile.

11. Malcolm Muggeridge, *Something Beautiful for God: Mother Teresa of Calcutta*, London: Collins, 1971, p 66.
12. From the Letter to Proba, in *Divine Office*, vol III, p 662.
13. In *Divine Office*, vol III, p 149*.

Prayer on the Mount of Olives

The whole teaching on prayer in Luke – as in Mark and Matthew – is personified in the example of Jesus at the end of his journey to Jerusalem. This is the Gethsemane prayer (Lk 22:39-46). Luke tells us that Jesus 'came out and went, as was his custom, to the Mount of Olives' (Lk 22:39). We should note the emphasis: it was his 'custom'. The word Luke uses denotes a religious custom (cf Lk 1:9; 2:42; Acts 6:14; 15:1). Jesus, as we have seen often before in Luke's gospel, used to go off to pray. But on this occasion, we are told that his disciples 'followed him' (Lk 22:39). Luke uses the technical term *akoloutheô*, meaning 'to follow Jesus as a disciple'. This, then, is Jesus' final invitation for all disciples to follow his example in prayer. It is noteworthy, too, that Jesus invites all his disciples to pray, and not just the three chosen ones, Peter, James and John, as in the other gospels (cf Mk 14:32; Mt 26:36). Again, the lesson of Jesus on prayer is, in Luke, for the whole community of the church.

Jesus addresses these words to his disciples: 'Pray that you may not come into the time of trial' (Lk 22:40). The original reads: 'Keep on praying that ...' The lesson is on persevering prayer – again a special feature of Luke's teaching on prayer (cf Lk 11:5-13; 18:1-8). Luke even repeats this lesson at the end of the scene. Jesus returns to his disciples, we are told, and says, 'Get up and pray' (Lk 22:46), that is, pray continually. Again, Luke is careful to tell us that Jesus, in his agony, 'prayed more earnestly' (Lk 22:44); he prayed not just once, but he kept on praying.

A special feature of Luke's gospel, as we have often seen, is not just the teachings of Jesus on prayer, but the witness of Jesus himself at prayer. This continues into the heart of the Gethsemane scene. So we notice that in Luke – unlike in Matthew and Mark – there is no triple departure of Jesus from his disciples. The whole scene unfolds after Jesus 'withdrew from them about a stone's throw' (Lk 22:41) – that is, still within earshot and visible to them. They were, all of them, witnesses to this lesson of Jesus on persevering prayer (cf Lk 1:2). It was a lesson for the whole church. It is also significant that Luke shows

Jesus kneeling to pray; Jesus does not fall on the ground in help-lessness as in Mark (Mk 14:35), or fall prostrate as in Matthew (Mt 26:39); rather, he 'knelt down, and prayed' (Lk 22:41).

We notice, too, how Luke's description can be understood in terms of the passion-resurrection of Jesus: 'When he got up from prayer, he came to the disciples and found them sleeping be-cause of grief, and he said to them, "Why are you sleeping? Get up and pray that you may not come into the time of trial"' (Lk 22:45-46). The New Testament often describes death as a 'sleep' (cf Mt 27:52; Jn 11:11; Acts 7:60; 13:36). At this point in Luke (Lk 22:45), the disciples are said to be literally 'dead asleep' (*koimô-menous*). By contrast, Jesus himself 'got up from prayer' and said to his disciples, 'Get up and pray' (Lk 22:45-46). The term used here for 'get up' is *anistêmi*, which is a word that frequently evokes the resurrection of Jesus.[14] It is the same lesson of Luke implied by the many prayer references throughout the journey of Jesus to Jerusalem: prayer forms part of that one great ascend-ing movement of Jesus to heaven through his passion-resurrec-tion.

A spiritual ascent

It is hardly surprising, then, if prayer is sometimes described as a 'lifting up of the mind to God'. Thomas Aquinas could think of no better definition, and he in turn simply borrowed it from John Damascene.[15] It is this same ascending movement which is reflected in the prayerful gesture of Jesus in the gospels as he often 'looked up to heaven' (Mk 6:41; 7:34; Jn 11:41; 17:1). But perhaps nobody has described the ascending movement of prayer better than Thérèse of Lisieux whose definition of prayer has found its way into the *Catechism of the Catholic Church*. She speaks of prayer as a heaven-directed impulse of the heart, a fling of the heart to the heart of God: 'For me, *prayer* is an aspir-ation of the heart, it is a simple glance directed to heaven, it is a

14. Cf Mk 8:31; Lk 18:33; 24:7; Jn 20:9.
15. John Damascene, *De Fide Orth*. III, 24: PG 94, 1089; quoted in Thomas Aquinas, *Summa Theologica* II-II q. 83 a. 1.

cry of gratitude and love in the midst of trial as well as joy'.[16] This ascent to God in prayer is no escape for us – nor was it for Thérèse – from the trials of daily living and the challenges of the Christian life. It contains the full import of Luke's understanding of prayer: the pain and the rejoicing, the dying and the rising – the oneness with Jesus Christ in his passion and resurrection.

16. Thérèse of Lisieux, *Story of a Soul, op. cit.*, p 242; cf *Catechism of the Catholic Church* #2558.

For Pondering and Prayer

QUESTIONS FOR REFLECTION

1. Prayer in Luke is closely linked with the Holy Spirit and with the establishment of the kingdom. In what way is this connected with the evangelist's broad vision of salvation history in his two-volume work, the gospel and Acts?

2. Luke's gospel is often referred to as *the* gospel of prayer. Why should this be so?

3. Jesus withdraws for quiet prayer more frequently in Luke than in the other gospels. What does this tell us about prayer, and are there any practical lessons to be learnt from this?

A GUIDED *LECTIO DIVINA*

Listening to the Word (Lk 10:38-42)
Now as they went on their way, he entered a certain village, where a woman named Martha welcomed him into her home. She had a sister named Mary, who sat at the Lord's feet and listened to what he was saying. But Martha was distracted by her many tasks; so she came to him and asked, 'Lord, do you not care that my sister has left me to do all the work by myself? Tell her then to help me.' But the Lord answered her, 'Martha, Martha, you are worried and distracted by many things; there is need of only one thing. Mary has chosen the better part, which will not be taken away from her.'

Reading
Relax. Invoke the Holy Spirit. Then read this passage slowly, attentively and reverently, with mind and heart open to receive the word, ready to respond to whatever it asks of you. Know that it is a word of love from God addressed to you personally. Reread it two or three times – calmly, quietly and without haste.

Meditation
Take a word or phrase from the reading that continues to linger in your mind. For example: 'Martha, Martha, you are worried and distracted by many things.' Put your own name in place of

Martha's. These are kind and gentle words of love to you too. Linger on them for a while. When Jesus spoke them, he was on his way to his death in Jerusalem. He had much reason to be worried. Yet he saw that all excessive anxiety is useless. How can we learn from him, in the midst of our own trials, to shed our anxieties and rest in his peace?

Mary sat at the Lord's feet and listened to his words. Can you recall any other time that Jesus spoke about listening to him? For example: 'Everyone who belongs to the truth listens to my voice' (Jn 18:37). Ponder deeply on these words. Think of someone who has listened attentively to you. How could you tell that they were listening at a deep level? Reflect on what this tells you about how to listen to Jesus.

Prayer

Lay your worries and anxieties before Jesus in prayer: 'Jesus, I know that I am often anxious and worried about many things. You were gentle with Martha; be gentle with me, too. I want to listen quietly and patiently to your word, like Mary. Help me to see that this is the most important activity in my daily life.' Be open before him, to receive his help.

Contemplation

Sit in stillness at the feet of Jesus, listening to what he has to say to you. He is directing your heart quietly and imperceptibly, and teaching you his wisdom through his word. He listened to his Father in silence – on the hillside, in solitude, and deep into the night. He is listening to you now. Continue to listen to him, letting the silence grow and deepen. Surrender yourself to his transforming power.

Action

Martha welcomed Jesus into her home. We can all feel drained at times when others make demands on us. We will easily find any number of excuses to complain like Martha. In future, try to welcome everyone with kindness, gentleness and understanding – knowing that the work is less important than the person.

CHAPTER 4

Praying with John

We now come to consider prayer in John – a gospel in which prayer reaches profound depths. The prayer focus is mainly on Jesus: on his communion with the Father. Nowhere is this more evident than in John 17, the priestly prayer of Jesus. This prayer not only represents the deepest insight into how Jesus prayed; it also draws together, in a gemlike synthesis, the major themes of the fourth gospel. It could, in fact, be called the whole of John's gospel in prayer form.[1] For this reason, this chapter will focus primarily on the priestly prayer.[2]

The inexhaustible treasures of this inspirational and complex prayer will take an eternity to unfold. But it is not my intention to offer a scholarly interpretation of it, verse by verse as in a commentary. Instead, I wish merely to suggest some of its diverse perspectives as a key to opening up its rich content – not only to know it better, but to pray it better. Firstly, though, by way of introduction, a brief survey of John's approach to prayer, in relation to that of the other gospels, will shed some light on the originality of John's contribution to the gospel tradition of prayer.

Climax of a tradition

The teaching of all four evangelists is firmly rooted in the same ever-deepening and ever-growing gospel tradition of prayer. However, John's gospel is strikingly different from the synoptics, and this is no less true of its treatment of prayer. In John,

1. This aspect of John 17 has been admirably treated by Eugene McCaffrey OCD, in his article 'God Speaking to God: A Gospel in Prayer', *Mount Carmel*, vol 51/4, 2003, pp 29-34.
2. For other aspects of prayer in John, see the following chapter, which focuses on the Holy Spirit in this gospel.

there is no mention of the solitary prayer of Jesus, for example, recorded so frequently in the other gospels. On one occasion, Jesus does slip off into the solitude of the hills, in response to a wave of popular enthusiasm and acclaim: 'When Jesus realised that they were about to come and take him by force to make him king, he withdrew again to the mountain by himself' (Jn 6:15). But there is no indication that he went off to pray.

Nor is there anything in John to compare with Mark's teaching on the prayer of faith (Mk 11:20-24); nothing, either, to resemble the catechetical instruction on prayer in Matthew (Mt 6:5-15); and certainly nothing to compare with prayer in Luke as a silent listening, exemplified repeatedly by the solitary prayer of Jesus (Lk 5:16; 6:12; 9:18; 11:1; cf 10:39). Neither is there any direct mention in John of the dispositions for prayer which are presented to us in the synoptics: humility (Lk 18:14), forgiveness (Mk 11:25; Mt 6:12, 14-15), perseverance (Lk 11:9-13; 18:1). In fact, this is hardly surprising. John's gospel, written some sixty years after the death of Jesus, is the last of the four, and all these facets of prayer were already deeply embedded in the gospel tradition and had been explored by the other evangelists. By the time John was writing, the church, under the action of the Holy Spirit, had already for over half a century penetrated prayerfully into the teaching of Jesus, and pondered deeply on the lessons of his teaching and his own example at prayer. John, in a real sense, is a culmination of the whole gospel tradition on prayer, a kind of climax or final word on the various perspectives opened up in the earlier gospels.

New perspectives

In the fourth gospel, Jesus rarely speaks explicitly about prayer, but he does speak of worship in his encounter with the Samaritan woman by Jacob's well: 'the hour is coming,' he says to her, 'and is now here, when the true worshippers will worship the Father in spirit and truth, for the Father seeks such as these to worship him. God is spirit, and those who worship him must worship in spirit and truth' (Jn 4:23-24). True Christian prayer, the fruit of authentic worship, is a movement of the Spirit centred on Jesus and directed entirely through him as the 'way' (Jn 14:6) to the Father who is the goal of all our deepest aspirations. As John later shows, the Son dwells with the Father and the Spirit in every believer (cf Jn 14:17, 23). The indwelling – the presence of God in our inner dwelling place – may therefore be seen as an expansion, in Trinitarian terms, of Matthew's teaching on the 'inner room' (Mt 6:6). This hidden and secret communion with God does not, though, diminish in any way the value of vocal prayer or external worship.

A characteristic of the fourth evangelist is to refer to prayer 'in the name'. This is a form of communing that speaks of deep and intimate prayer in union with the person of Jesus: 'I will do whatever you ask in my name, so that the Father may be glorified in the Son. If in my name you ask me for anything, I will do it' (Jn 14:13-14; cf 15:16; 16:23, 26). Here, there is the promise of an infallible response to prayer, and this in fact has its roots in the earlier gospels: 'Again, truly I tell you, if two of you agree on earth about anything you ask, it will be done for you by my Father in heaven. For where two or three are gathered in my name, I am there among them' (Mt 18:19-20).[3]

But most striking of all, perhaps, is John's treatment of the Gethsemane scene; in fact, the scene as such, which is of paramount importance in the other gospels, appears at first sight to be absent in John (cf Mt 26:36-46; Mk 14:32-42; Lk 22:39-46). It is, however, implicit in the words of Jesus shortly before his passion: 'Now my soul is troubled. And what should I say – "Father, save me from this hour"? No, it is for this reason that I have come to this hour. Father, glorify your name' (Jn 12:27).[4] These words are not spoken in a garden, and there is no mention here of the three privileged witnesses to the scene, no sleep of

---

3. Cf Mt 7:7-11; Mk 11:23-24; Lk 11:5-13.
4. Brown writes: 'The closest parallel to the Synoptic agony scene in Jn is 12:23, 27-30, and it is curious that it is there we have the Johannine parallel to the first petition of the [Our Father] ("Father, glorify your name").' See his 'The Pater Noster', *op. cit.*, p 191, note 67 and his 'Incidents that are Units', *op. cit.*

the disciples, no sweat of blood, no explicit surrender of Jesus in his agony. But we will discover later that reflection on these words of John reveals a whole new perspective for a deeper and more fruitful understanding of the richness of the Gethsemane scene described extensively in the other gospels.

A seamless robe

In spite of the differences between the fourth gospel and the synoptics, there is a close link between John and Luke. This is also true of their approach to prayer. In the prayer of Jesus there is an ascending movement. In Luke, Jesus is described at the ascension as 'lifting up his hands' (Lk 24:50) in a prayerful gesture to bless his disciples; and 'while he was blessing them, he withdrew from them and was carried up into heaven' (Lk 24:51). In John, prayer is intimately linked with a similar and symbolic gesture of Jesus which speaks volumes about his prayer as a heaven-directed glance to his Father: 'Jesus looked upward' as he prayed at the tomb of Lazarus (Jn 11:41). He repeats the gesture by way of prelude to his final prayer at the supper, when again 'he looked upward' and spoke to his heavenly Father (Jn 17:1). However, there is another dimension to this ascent. We notice, first, that the passion-resurrection of Jesus is described, in Luke, as a 'taking up' (Lk 9:51; cf 24:51; Acts 1:9.11); and we see, too, that in John all three predictions of the passion-resurrection are referred to as a 'lifting up' (Jn 3:14; 8:28; 12:32). The priestly prayer is nothing less than a prayer of Jesus already ascending to his Father through his passion-resurrection, in anticipation of the event.

In John, as in Luke, there is an important link between prayer and the coming of the kingdom. Luke presents Jesus alone, in quiet communion with his Father, at the great turning-points in the unfolding of God's plan of redemption (Lk 3:21; 6:12; 9:18, 28-29; 11:1). During the last supper in John, Jesus prays for the fulfilment of God's plan, the unity and love that herald the coming of the kingdom: 'that they may all be one ... completely one' (Jn 17:21, 23); 'that the love with which you have loved me may

be in them, and I in them' (Jn 17:26). Another similarity between
the two gospels is that Luke refers to the passion-death of Jesus
as the 'hour': 'This is your hour, and the power of darkness!' (Lk
22:53). The priestly prayer in John is the prayer of this same
'hour' and begins with the words: 'Father, the hour has come'
(Jn 17:1; cf 12:27). This mysterious 'hour' is a pervading theme of
the fourth gospel. For John, it is an 'hour' of glory.

Again, this link between prayer and glory is already highly
significant in Luke's description of the Tabor scene: Jesus 'went
up on the mountain to pray,' we are told, and was transfigured
'while he was praying', and the disciples 'saw his glory' (Lk
9:28-32). In his priestly prayer in John, Jesus links his own glory
with that of his Father: 'Father ... glorify your Son so that the
Son may glorify you' (Jn 17:1). All these disparate elements in
Luke – ascending movement, plan of salvation, the hour, and
glory – are scattered throughout the gospel of John and woven
together like so many strands into the seamless robe of Jesus'
final prayer. As we have already observed, the priestly prayer of
Jesus may be described as the whole gospel of John in prayer
form.

A gathering of the nations

As the last of the gospels John is, we have seen, the culmination
of a gospel tradition. But he is heir to the whole biblical tradition, too. The mind of John was steeped in the long tradition of
the people of God, and his gospel echoes continually with reson-
ances of the Old Testament.

There is a biblical source that can help us to clarify the dy-
namics of Jesus' final prayer in John: a constant movement to
and fro, a two-way traffic, so to speak. The light of the word of
God emanates *from* the Father through Jesus, and the believer in
turn responds through Jesus back *towards* the Father. As we read
in the priestly prayer: 'The words that you [Father] gave to me I
have given to them, and they have received them and know in
truth that I came from you; and they have believed that you sent
me' (Jn 17:8). It is worth considering the prayer against the back-

ground of one of the great central texts of Isaiah, and indeed of the Old Testament, where there is this same two-way movement. This is when the prophet describes the final unfolding of God's plan of redemption as the light of God's word emanating from the temple, and the pilgrimage of all people streaming towards the temple:

> In days to come the mountain of the Lord's house shall be established as the highest of the mountains, and shall be raised above the hills; all the nations shall stream to it. Many peoples shall come and say, 'Come, let us go up to the mountain of the Lord, to the house of the God of Jacob; that he may teach us his ways and that we may walk in his paths.' For out of Zion shall go forth instruction, and the word of the Lord from Jerusalem ... O house of Jacob, come, let us walk in the light of the Lord! (Is 2:2-3, 5; cf Mic 4:1-2, 5)

Here, then, we notice not just a movement to the temple; there is also a movement from the temple – a movement to and fro. Isaiah depicts the temple as the goal to which all the nations of the world ascend in pilgrimage, like a great new exodus and a homecoming of the nations at the end of time. But at the same time, 'instruction' and 'the word' emanate from this same temple, radiating from it like a beacon of light to guide the nations to the goal of salvation: 'For out of Zion shall go forth instruction, and the word of the Lord from Jerusalem ... come, let us walk in the light of the Lord!'

In the psalms, too, there is the same double movement, to and fro. The psalmist portrays a whole people in exile, yearning for the promised land: 'By the rivers of Babylon there we sat and wept, remembering Sion' (Ps 136:1). This is echoed by his own pilgrim's prayer, as he longs for access to God in the temple: 'How lovely is your dwelling place, Lord, God of hosts. My soul is longing and yearning, is yearning for the courts of the Lord' (Ps 83:2-3). Not only does the psalmist in exile long to journey to the temple, but he also prays: 'O send forth your light and your truth; let these be my guide. Let them bring me to your holy mountain to the place where you dwell. And I will come to the altar of God, the God of my joy' (Ps 42:3-4). This, then, is our twofold movement. For there, in God's temple, the light of truth burns brightly and radiates from it to guide the pilgrim safely home.

Echoes of an ancient prayer tradition

In the Old Testament, we find two important prayers which bear a significant resemblance to the priestly prayer of Jesus. They provide us with a pattern for the arrangement or structure of this prayer in John. In each case there is a simple, though significant, threefold division.

One of these prayers occurs at the dedication of the temple in the First Book of Kings. Here, Solomon prays with a remarkable breadth of vision (1 Kgs 8:12-53; cf Chron 6:1-42). He intercedes for *himself* and for *the people of Israel*: 'Let your eyes be open to the plea of your servant, and to the plea of your people Israel, listening to them whenever they call to you' (1 Kgs 8:52). But Solomon, in this prayer, pleads not just for himself and for his own people. The sweep of his prayer reaches far beyond national confines, as he prays for 'foreigners', *those who are not part of the people of God*:

> Likewise when a foreigner, who is not of your people Israel, comes from a distant land because of your name – for they shall hear of your great name, your mighty hand, and your outstretched arm – when a foreigner comes and prays toward this house, then hear in heaven your dwelling place, and do according to all that the foreigner calls to you, so that all the peoples of the earth may know your name and fear you, as do your people Israel ... (1 Kgs 8:41-43)

We find a similar, all-embracing, pattern in the priestly prayer of Jesus. He prays for *himself*, for the close circle of his own *disciples* and for the wider community of *all believers*. So firstly, he prays for his own glorification through his passion-resurrection: 'Father ... glorify your Son ... glorify me in your own presence with the glory that I had in your presence before the world existed' (Jn 17:1, 5). Jesus then prays for his immediate followers whom he has chosen from among the people of God to be the nucleus of the new community of believers: 'I am asking on their behalf ... protect them in your name ... sanctify them in the truth' (Jn 17:9, 11, 17). Finally, the prayer of Jesus takes on a universal dimension. It stretches far beyond the little band of his disciples to embrace the new people of God, all future believers: 'I ask not only on behalf of these [disciples], but also on behalf of those who will believe in me through their word' (Jn 17:20).

Thus the prayer of Solomon provides us – and possibly provided John – with a model for a division of the prayer of Jesus into three parts, as Jesus intercedes for himself (vv 1-5), for his disciples (vv 6-19), and for the universal community of all believers (vv 20-26). This is a simple threefold structure, helping us to follow more easily the gradual expanding outreach of the priestly prayer of Jesus.

A prayer of atonement

An even more striking parallel with the priestly prayer in John is the ritual of atonement in the Old Testament. Once a year on Yom Kippur, the Day of Atonement, the high priest entered the Holy of Holies, the inner sanctuary behind the veil, to stand before the presence of God, making intercession for sin (Lev 16). Like Solomon in his great prayer at the dedication of the temple, the high priest interceded for three groups of people, creating an ever-widening outreach: *himself*, his *household*, and the *whole community of Israel*. So, too, as we have seen, Jesus prays for three parallel concerns: for *himself* – 'Father ... glorify your Son' (cf Jn 17:1-5); for his *disciples* – 'those whom you [Father] gave me' (cf Jn 17:6-19); and for the *wider community of the church* – 'those who will believe in me through [the disciples'] word' (cf Jn 17:20-26). The gradual expanding movement of Jesus' prayer ultimately extends to embrace the whole world.

But the term 'atonement' – its meaning in English quite literally 'at-one-ment' – does not refer only to prayer of intercession:

it also involves sacrifice. The priestly prayer of Jesus is a great prayer of intercession, but right at the heart of it – or, we might say, at the crucial turning-point in the prayer – Jesus speaks in equivalent terms of his own sacrificial self-offering: 'for their sakes I sanctify myself' (Jn 17:19). Here, 'sanctify' (*hagiazô*), which designates in the Greek to take something out of profane usage and to hand it over to God, also takes on a sacrificial import (cf Deut 15:19-21).[5] But Jesus' prayer of self-offering takes on a significance far beyond the offering of animals by the Jewish high priest on the Day of Atonement (cf Lev 16). Jesus here is handing himself over to his Father as a sacrificial victim. The priestly prayer is the enactment in prayer of the sacrificial movement of redemption for sin. The return of Jesus to his Father makes possible an 'at-one-ment' of Jesus with all believers: 'that they may be one, as we are one, I in them and you in me' (Jn 17:22-23). So, Jesus stands before the face of God as the great mediator or priest, that is, 'pontifex' or 'bridge-builder' (from *pons*, 'bridge' and *facere*, 'to make'). He builds a bridge of reconciliation between God and his people, interceding for all believers, sacrificing himself for them, carrying them in his heart and presenting them before the throne of God.

A gospel of revelation

Everything in John's gospel is focused on the person of Jesus as the Word made flesh who is the Truth, or revelation of his Father. This is the central insight of his gospel (cf Jn 14:6; 1:14; Heb 1:2). That is not to say that Jesus is the revelation of God in this gospel only. In John, revelation is linked to prayer, as in Matthew and Luke: 'I thank you, Father, Lord of heaven and earth … no one knows the Son except the Father, and no one knows the Father except the Son and anyone to whom the Son chooses to reveal him' (Mt 11:25, 27; cf Lk 10:21-22). It is hardly surprising that these words, as we have seen, are often aptly re-

---

5. Commenting on John's gospel, Cyril of Alexandria writes: '[Christ] said, "I make myself holy", meaning "I consecrate and offer myself as a spotless sacrifice with a sweet savour." In *Divine Office*, vol II, p 551.

ferred to as a 'saying of John' – technically, a 'Johannine *logion*'. But while these words are isolated instances in Matthew and Luke, the fourth gospel is *the* gospel of revelation. We have only to look, for example, at a central verse of John's prologue (Jn 1:1-18), which is like a replica in miniature of his whole gospel. Right at the heart of it, we find the words: 'And the Word became flesh and lived among us [literally: 'pitched his tent among us'], and we have seen his glory, the glory as of a father's only son, full of grace and truth' (Jn 1:14; cf 14:6). 'Grace and truth' relate back to an Old Testament phrase, *hesed we 'emeth* (Ps 39:11) – meaning 'love and fidelity' – which designates God's constant, abiding love. Indeed, 'truth' in John is not an abstract concept. It is love manifested in Jesus as the new tabernacle or temple: it is God dwelling among his people.

We remember that the prologue reaches a climax with these words: 'No one has ever seen God. It is God the only Son, who is close to the Father's heart, who has made him known' (Jn 1:18). But that is not exactly what John is saying here. He says literally, 'has made known' or 'has revealed' (*exêgêsato*). There is no direct object: no 'him'. The evangelist fixes our attention, not on the content of revelation, but on the person of Jesus as the one who reveals. He is the revelation of God, the truth of God's love in person. The Letter to the Hebrews expresses the same idea: 'In these last days [God] has spoken to us by a Son' (Heb 1:2). Again, there is no direct object. We are not told what Jesus has spoken: there is nothing about the content of the message. The essential point is that God has revealed: he has spoken in the person of his Son.

A prayer of revelation

We can now see how the priestly prayer of Jesus is intimately linked with the central insight of John's gospel: Jesus is the revelation, in person, of the Father. The First Letter of John expresses this idea perfectly and is captured here beautifully in the translation of Ronald Knox:

Our message concerns that Word, who is life; what he was

from the first, what we have heard about him, what our own eyes have seen of him; what it was that met our gaze, and the touch of our hands. Yes, life dawned; and it is as eyewitnesses that we give you news of that life, that eternal life, which ever abode with the Father and has dawned, now, on us. (1 Jn 1:1-2)

Into that life we are drawn, by faith in the Word who is the revelation of God – into that inner life of love in God, into what John calls 'fellowship (*koinônia*) ... with the Father and with his Son Jesus Christ' (1 Jn 1:3). Revelation in John is not just about revealing an abstract truth, or even a series of truths. It is, first and foremost, God revealing himself in love and we, in return, giving ourselves to him in love, through faith in his word and through prayer. In this way, we enter into eternal life and share the inner life of love in the heart of the Trinity. This is something that Jesus prays for in his priestly prayer: 'That those also, whom you have given me, may be with me where I am' (Jn 17:24). And Jesus is explicit: 'I am in the Father ... The Father and I are one' (Jn 10:38, 30).

The vocabulary of revelation pervades the priestly prayer. Jesus speaks about the truth: 'Sanctify them in the truth; your word is truth' (Jn 17:17). He also refers to revelation as his words: 'The words that you gave to me I have given to them, and they have received them ... and they have believed' (Jn 17:8); ultimately, all these 'words' are reduced to the one 'word' of revelation: 'They have kept your word' (Jn 17:6). Jesus speaks especially of making the Father known: 'I made your name known to them, and I will make it known' (Jn 17:26; cf 17:6, 14). Jesus faces his passion-death, 'knowing that the Father had given all things into his hands' (Jn 13:3). All these gifts – Jesus' words, his name, his glory, his disciples – are not his own, he tells us in this prayer, but have been given to him by the Father (Jn 17:2, 6-9, 11-12, 22, 24). The Father is all-giving. That is why his name is 'Love'. He is always giving himself.

A prayer for unity
This central insight – of Jesus as the revelation of the Father – is

inseparably linked by John with the lesson of universal salvation. Only in the fourth gospel do we find these words of Jesus: 'I am the light of the world' (Jn 8:12; 9:5). Not just a light for the people of Israel, but a light for all, for the whole world. John dramatises this great truth for us in that lovely scene by Jacob's Well.[6] At the end of the conversation, the Samaritan woman left Jesus and 'went back to the city' (Jn 4:28) to share the good news with her fellow townsfolk. John tells us that they, in turn, 'left the city and were on their way to [Jesus]' (Jn 4:30). We can see them there in the background, like an unending procession, coming to Jesus. At the same time, in the front of the stage, we see Jesus talking to his disciples. He speaks of God's design as a 'harvest-reaping' and the accomplishment of his will as the work of his Father (Jn 4:31-35). The scene then reaches a climax. The Samaritans come to Jesus and say to the woman: 'It is no longer because of what you said that we believe, for we have heard for ourselves, and we know that this is truly the Saviour of the world' (Jn 4:42) – the Saviour of all people.

A pilgrim's prayer
There is a telling example of irony in John, when even the Jewish authorities themselves, the enemies of Jesus, unwittingly proclaim the message of salvation for all: 'Look, the world has gone after him!' (Jn 12:19). Immediately, there follows what appears to be an insignificant scene. Some Greeks on pilgrimage to Jerusalem want to have access to Jesus (Jn 12:20-22). These people, who represent the pagan world, say: 'We wish to see Jesus' (Jn 12:21). No answer is given; that is, no direct answer. In fact, there is an answer, an indirect answer: 'The hour has come,' Jesus says, 'for the Son of Man to be glorified' (Jn 12:23). It is only through the passion-resurrection of Jesus – what John calls his glorification (Jn 12:28; cf 7:39; 13:31-32) – that the Gentile world will have access to Jesus. The scene concludes with the marvellous words: 'And I, when I am lifted up from the earth, will

6. Treated more extensively in the following chapter, section 'A prayer dialogue'.

draw all people to myself' (Jn 12:32). In this way, Isaiah's description of the nations on pilgrimage to the Jerusalem temple at the end of time will be fulfilled (cf Is 2:2-3, 5; Mic 4:1-2).[7]

John, however, gives his own particular slant to this theme of universal salvation. It becomes a kind of gathering into one of all believers through the passion and resurrection of Jesus. The prophetic words of the high priest, Caiaphas, highlight this special aspect: 'It is better for you to have one man die for the people than to have the whole nation destroyed' (Jn 11:50). Then, John hastens to comment: 'He did not say this on his own, but being high priest that year he prophesied that Jesus was about to die for the nation, and not for the nation only, but to gather into one the dispersed children of God' (Jn 11:51-52; cf 18:14).

The central theme of John's gospel, then, is twofold: that Jesus is the revelation, in person, of the Father; and, closely linked with it, the truth of universal redemption. In equivalent Johannine terms, this means the gathering into one of all believers through the passion and resurrection. It is this unity that Jesus longs for in his priestly prayer: unity for the disciples among themselves – 'so that they may be one, as we are one' (Jn 17:11); and likewise among all believers – 'that they may all be one' (Jn 17:21). But also, unity for all disciples and believers with the Father through Jesus: 'As you, Father, are in me and I am in you, may they also be in us ... that they may be one, as we are one, I in them and you in me, that they may become completely one' (Jn 17:21-23). The unity in this prayer serves admirably to stress the intimacy of the believer's union with Jesus: in him, all believers are one with each other; and through him, they are one with the Father. Ultimately, Jesus is the high priest, the mediator between ourselves and God.

A timeless prayer

John introduces the priestly prayer with the simple phrase:

7. For a detailed analysis of the links between Isaiah 2:2-3, 5 and the pilgrimage of the Greeks in John 12:20ff, see James McCaffrey OCD, *The House with Many Rooms: The Temple Theme of Jn 14,2-3, Analecta Biblica* 114, Rome: Editrice Pontificio Istituto Biblico, 1988, pp 201-2.

'After Jesus had spoken these words' (Jn 17:1). This phrase links the prayer directly with what Jesus has just said at the supper: 'I have said this to you, so that in me you may have peace. In the world you face persecution. But take courage; I have conquered the world!' (Jn 16:33). The victory of Jesus through his passion-resurrection is considered here both as a past event and also as one which is present, here and now. That is the meaning of the phrase 'have conquered' in the original text – carrying both past and present. But John's expression of 'having' conquered also carries implications for the future, in terms of a continuing effect.[8] This, too, is the perspective of the prayer: in one sense, Jesus has not yet, in time, fully completed his work of redemption – the passion-resurrection has yet to follow – but the effect of it is, in some mysterious sense, already present, here and now, and for all time.

It is significant that if we remove that single link-phrase, 'After Jesus had spoken these words', the priestly prayer of Jesus could stand almost anywhere in the gospel of John, in isolation. The prayer has a timeless quality all of its own. This helps to explain at least one curious feature of the prayer, which also reflects the timelessness of the passion-resurrection: the merging of past, present and future. The prayer ranges to and fro from one time sequence to another: 'I have made your name known' in the past (Jn 17:6, 26); 'I am coming to you' in the present (Jn 17:11, 13); 'I will make [your name] known' in the future (Jn 17:26).

The moment of supreme importance at the centre of salvation history is when Jesus goes to his Father through his passion-resurrection. It is a timeless 'now' (Jn 13:31) where the temporal and the eternal fuse. It is always present and gives to the whole sequence of time – past, present and future – a perennial value. Jesus is crossing the threshold of eternity through his passion-resurrection and entering into communion with his Father, taking with him all believers, for we are all included in this prayer.

---

8. The perfect tense in the original Greek indicates that the action continues.

The paschal mystery is fixed forever, as it were, in the prayer of Jesus. It is at the centre of time, and yet in a sense it stands above time. But, for all that, it is always present in time and until the end of time. It is what John refers to in his gospel as the 'hour'. At the outset of his prayer, Jesus reminds us: 'The hour has come' (Jn 17:1).

A prayer of the new exodus

We first hear of the 'hour' at Cana: 'My hour has not yet come' (Jn 2:4). It is a future, mysterious 'hour'. No further details are given here. Then, when Jesus speaks to the Samaritan woman, we learn that it is an 'hour' that is already present: 'The hour is coming, and is now here' (Jn 4:23; cf 4:21; 5:25; 16:32). Later, we are told that it is the 'hour' of a general resurrection: 'The hour is coming when all who are in their graves will hear his voice and will come out' (Jn 5:28-29). At the heart of the gospel, we are reminded again that 'his hour had not yet come' (Jn 7:30; 8:20). The passion draws ever closer, and we learn that it is linked with the glorification of Jesus: 'The hour has come for the Son of Man to be glorified' (Jn 12:23). It is to be an 'hour' of danger. Jesus prays: 'Father, save me from this hour' (Jn 12:27). On the eve of his passion, Jesus describes it as the hour of his exodus: 'Before the festival of the Passover, Jesus knew that his hour had come to depart from this world and go to the Father' (Jn 13:1). This is the 'hour' of the new passover, the new exodus, the 'hour' of the glorification of Jesus through his passion-resurrection.

This is also the perspective in the priestly prayer. Jesus prays for his own glorification and for that of his Father through the passion-resurrection: 'Glorify your Son so that the Son may glorify you ... I glorified you on earth ... So now, Father, glorify me ... with the glory that I had in your presence before the world existed' (Jn 17:1, 4-5). He also prays that all believers may share in that glory: 'The glory that you have given me I have given them ... Father, I desire that those also, whom you have given me, may ... see my glory' (Jn 17:22, 24). It is the prayer of the 'hour' as Jesus strides across the threshold of eternity, on his

way – his passover – to the Father: 'I am no longer in the world
… I am coming to you' (Jn 17:11, 13). Jesus is the mediator, the
high priest. And it is as such that he prays. This prayer has been
rightly called the 'priestly prayer' of Jesus. What Jesus is accom-
plishing here and now himself, as he enters into union with his
Father through his passion-resurrection, is what Jesus prays
may, in turn, be realised in every believer until the end of time.

A prayer for sanctification

Earlier at the supper, Jesus promised that he would pray for the
Holy Spirit to come upon his disciples. His words are explicit: 'I
will ask the Father, and he will give you another Advocate, to be
with you forever. This is the Spirit of truth' (Jn 14:16-17). The
Paraclete is also referred to explicitly as 'the Holy Spirit' (Jn
14:26). Even though there is no explicit reference to the Spirit in
the priestly prayer itself, the action of the Spirit pervades it – the
Spirit who not only reveals and unifies but also sanctifies.

At what can be taken as a turning-point of the prayer, Jesus
says: 'Sanctify them in the truth; your word is truth … And for
their sakes I sanctify myself, so that they also may be sanctified
in truth' (Jn 17:17, 19). As we have seen, to sanctify means to take
out of profane usage and to hand over to God. Jesus asks his
Father to preserve the disciples from the world. In John, 'the
world' has many different meanings. In its most positive sense,
it refers to those who are the object of God's special love: 'God so
loved the world that he gave his only Son' (Jn 3:16). It can also
designate the created universe: 'Father, glorify me in your own
presence with the glory that I had in your presence before the
world existed' (Jn 17:5; cf 17:24). But in addition, it can refer in a
negative way to the world of darkness, or evil, the realm of
Satan. It is in this sense that Jesus prays to the Father to preserve
the disciples from the world. And he says to them: 'If you belonged to the world, the world would love you as its own.
Because you do not belong to the world, but I have chosen you
out of the world – therefore the world hates you' (Jn 15:19). Jesus
prays that his disciples may be sanctified, taken out of the world

of darkness: 'I have made your name known to those whom you gave me from the world … I am not asking on behalf of the world, but on behalf of those whom you gave me … the world has hated them because they do not belong to the world, just as I do not belong to the world … I ask you to protect them from the evil one' (Jn 17:6, 9, 14, 15). This is the work of the sanctifying Spirit.

A sacrificial prayer

But to sanctify, as we have seen, also has a sacrificial import. Jesus has already spoken earlier in the gospel about his self-giving sacrifice of the passion: 'I am the good shepherd … And I lay down my life for the sheep' (Jn 10:14-15). We find the same sacrificial import in the words of Jesus promising the gift of the Eucharist: 'The bread that I will give for the life of the world is my flesh' (Jn 6:51). The priestly prayer of Jesus lays bare the spontaneous and free surrender of Jesus to his Father in his passion, as he had previously explained it to his disciples: 'For this reason the Father loves me, because I lay down my life in order to take it up again … I lay it down of my own accord … I have received this command from my Father' (Jn 10:17-18). Jesus sanctifies himself in the priestly prayer as he moves out of this world and hands himself over to his Father in a sacrificial giving of himself through his passion-resurrection.

Jesus does not, however, sanctify himself alone. He also sanctifies his disciples: 'For their sakes I sanctify myself, so that they also may be sanctified in truth' (Jn 17:19). But the prayer of Jesus extends far beyond his disciples, to embrace all future believers 'who will believe in [Jesus] through [the disciples'] word' (Jn 17:20). Jesus prays that all believers may be taken out of the world of darkness and handed over to the Father. In a word, be sanctified. It is the work of the Spirit whom the Father will send in Jesus' name – 'the Holy Spirit,' Jesus says, reminding us that the Paraclete is the Spirit of holiness (Jn 14:26). The risen Jesus launches the church on its sanctifying mission of forgiveness in the power of that same Spirit: 'Receive the Holy Spirit. If you

forgive the sins of any, they are forgiven them' (Jn 20:22-23). It is
the Spirit who sanctifies.

A prayer for the fulfilment of God's plan

The ultimate goal expressed in the priestly prayer of Jesus is the
fulfilment of God's plan: 'Father, I desire that those also, whom
you have given me, may be with me where I am' (Jn 17:24; cf
14:3). This design of God has its own peculiar features in John.
The disciples are a gift to Jesus, given to him by the Father: 'This
is the will of him who sent me, that I should lose nothing of all
that he has given me' (Jn 6:39). The disciples are drawn to Jesus
by the Father: 'No one can come to me unless drawn by the
Father who sent me' (Jn 6:44). And Jesus, in turn, receives his
disciples from the Father and draws them to himself: 'And I,
when I am lifted up from the earth, will draw all people to myself' (Jn 12:32). John refers to the passion-resurrection as an indi-
visible movement of exaltation or ascent, two facets of the one
great event (cf Jn 12:32; 3:14; 8:28). Jesus' disciples are drawn to
him by the Father, received by Jesus through his passion-resurrection, and through Jesus given back to the Father. Such is the
plan of redemption in John.

We have a beautiful illustration of this Johannine slant in the
call of the first disciples (Jn 1:35-39). The account in John is very
different from that of the other gospels. The disciples are introduced to Jesus by the Baptist: 'Look, here is the Lamb of God!'
(Jn 1:36). They follow Jesus. Then Jesus turns round and sees
them already following him and says, 'What are you looking
for?' (Jn 1:38). Before they ever encounter Jesus personally, they
are already seeking, already being drawn to Jesus by the Father.
John expresses the same idea again, in a different way. The good
shepherd enters into the sheepfold and the sheep recognise his
voice. They listen to him because they already 'belong to the
truth' (Jn 18:37): they have been given by the Father to Jesus,
drawn to Jesus by the Father. Through his passion-resurrection,
Jesus receives the sheep from his Father and draws them to himself.

Again, the call of the first disciples illustrates the goal of God's plan. John frequently uses a subtle device of question and answer when he wants to open up a deeper sense of the gospel message. The disciples ask, 'Where are you staying?' (Jn 1:38), literally: 'remaining' or 'dwelling' (*menô*). In this first encounter, the term 'remain' – often translated as 'stay' or 'live' – is used three times for emphasis (Jn 1:38-39). Its deeper meaning gradually unfolds throughout the gospel: the Spirit remains in Jesus (Jn 1:32-33), the Spirit remains in the disciples (Jn 14:17), the Father remains in Jesus (Jn 14:10), the disciples remain in Jesus (Jn 6:56), and Jesus remains in the disciples (Jn 15:4). To 'remain', then, designates the perfect communion of all people with God, the unity expressed in the priestly prayer: 'I in them and you in me' (Jn 17:23).

A prayer for glory

The term 'remain' is characteristic of John to describe the profound mystery of the inner life of the Trinity and the sharing in it of believers. On the eve of his passion, Jesus describes his Father's heavenly dwelling as the place 'where I am' (Jn 14:3) and promises that he will come and take his disciples to himself so that they may dwell in it: 'In my Father's house there are many dwelling places … And if I go and prepare a place for you, I will come again and will take you to myself, so that where I am, there you may be also' (Jn 14:2-3). In his priestly prayer, Jesus echoes those words when he describes the goal of the plan of redemption: 'That they also may be with me where I am' (Jn 17:24). It is the climax to the whole theme of unity running through the priestly prayer. Believers are destined, in fulfilment of Jesus' prayer, to enter into the family of God where Jesus is one with the Father. In John, this is the unifying role of the Spirit by whom Jesus, when 'lifted up from the earth, will draw all people to [himself]' (Jn 12:32) and 'gather into one the dispersed children of God' (Jn 11:52).

In his priestly prayer, Jesus also explains the purpose of union between God and his people, in the divine plan: that they may 'see my glory, which you have given me because you loved me before the foundation of the world' (Jn 17:24). This glory is God's holiness revealed,[9] the visible manifestation of him who is 'the Holy One' (Is 40:25; Jer 50:29), the transcendent and totally 'Other' who cannot give his glory to another: 'Not to us, Lord, not to us, but to your name give the glory' (Ps 113[B]:1). In the priestly prayer, that glory is closely linked with the eternal love of the Father for Jesus. The word made flesh manifests that same glory. 'We have seen his glory, the glory as of a father's only son,' John tells us, 'full of grace and truth' (Jn 1:14): that is, full of God's 'abiding, constant or enduring love' – his saving love. The vision of God's glory is not, however, something that we must wait to experience only at the end of time. What Jesus asks for in his priestly prayer is already ours, through faith, revealed in the face of Christ: 'the glory of God' (cf 2 Cor 4:6). And Jesus has already given this glory to his disciples: 'The glory that you have given me I have given them, so that they may be one, as we are one' (Jn 17:22).

A prayer of reciprocal love

The final verse of the priestly prayer opens with the words: 'I made your name known to them, and I will make it known' (Jn 17:26). This theme of making the Father known was also there at the beginning of the prayer (Jn 17:6). This is hardly surprising for, as we have seen, Jesus as the revelation, in person, of the Father is the central insight of John's gospel. 'Whoever has seen me has seen the Father' (Jn 14:9), Jesus says. The gospel of John is the gospel of revelation. The sentence 'I made your name known' sums up the whole ministry of Jesus. It is a work of revelation. Jesus is 'the Word' (Jn 1:1) and 'the light of the world' (Jn 8:12; 9:5). In his self-giving love, Jesus has made known the Father's name. And it is a reciprocal love, as the Father, in turn,

---

9. Cf *Catechism of the Catholic Church* #2809; Is 6:3. Ernst Lohmeyer expresses this admirably: 'God's glory is His revealed holiness; His holiness is His hidden glory', as quoted in Brown, 'The Pater Noster', *op. cit.*, p 186, note 46.

gives himself in love to his Son: 'The Father loves the Son and has placed all things in his hands ... The Father loves the Son and shows him all that he himself is doing ... For this reason the Father loves me, because I lay down my life ... I have received this command from my Father' (Jn 3:35; 5:20; 10:17, 18). Jesus faces his passion 'so that the world may know that I love the Father' (Jn 14:31). The eternal flow of love between the Father and Son in the inner life of God is projected onto the stage of time in this to-ing and fro-ing of love between Jesus and his Father.

But Jesus also assures us that he will continue to reveal the Father's name in the future: 'I will make it known' (Jn 17:26). How? Through the Spirit. Jesus has just told his disciples at the supper that he will send 'another Advocate' to replace himself: 'the Spirit of truth' to remain with his disciples forever and to be in them (Jn 14:16-17). He explains to them the future revealing action of the Spirit: 'But the Advocate ... will teach you every-thing, and remind you of all that I have said to you' (Jn 14:26); and he adds further: 'When the Spirit of truth comes, he will guide you into all the truth' (Jn 16:12). Why this revelation? Jesus explains: 'That the love with which [the Father has] loved me may be in [the disciples], and I in them' (Jn 17:26). Revelation here is directed to communication: God communicates, gives himself by the revelation of the truth, gives his life and his love. This is the work of the revealing Spirit whom John calls 'the Spirit of truth' (Jn 14:17; 15:26; 16:13).

A prayer of the 'hour'

We have already mentioned that John's gospel contains an equivalent of the Gethsemane prayer in the synoptics: 'Now my soul is troubled. And what should I say – "Father, save me from this hour"? No, it is for this reason that I have come to this hour. Father, glorify your name' (Jn 12:27-28). Here, at least implicitly, there is a hint of the anguish emphasised more strongly in the other gospels: 'Now my soul is troubled' (Jn 12:27; cf Mt 26:38-39; Mk 14:33-35; Lk 22:42). It would also seem that in John, too,

Jesus accepts his Father's will gradually: 'Father, save me from this hour,' he says (Jn 12:27), echoing the cry of Jesus in Mark (Mk 14:36). Unlike the other gospels, however, Jesus' prayer in agony is linked explicitly with his glorification: 'Father,' Jesus prays, 'glorify your name' (Jn 12:28). The mention of 'hour' and 'glorification' stamp this prayer with two of the most striking features of the fourth gospel. They also link it closely with the priestly prayer. There, Jesus prays at the outset: 'Father, the hour has come' (Jn 17:1). This, as we have seen, is the 'hour' of Jesus' return to his Father through his passion-resurrection. The tension mounts with repeated mention of this 'hour' (Jn 2:4; 7:30; 8:20; 12:27) and reaches a climax in the whole dramatic movement of the fourth gospel when Jesus announces, at the beginning of the priestly prayer: 'The hour has come' (Jn 17:1).

This 'hour', then, is the hour of the glorification of Jesus. His glory was already visible in the 'Word made flesh': 'We have seen his glory, the glory as of a father's only son' (Jn 1:14). Jesus manifested it again at Cana: he 'revealed his glory', we are told, 'and his disciples believed in him' (Jn 2:11). During the feast of tabernacles, the glory of Jesus is identified with the passion-resurrection of Jesus: 'As yet there was no Spirit, because Jesus was not yet glorified' (Jn 7:39). As his ministry draws to a close, Jesus says: 'The hour has come for the Son of Man to be glorified' (Jn 12:23). Again, at the supper, as we have seen, he speaks of his glorification and that of his Father in him, through the passion-resurrection, as though it had already taken place: 'Now the Son of Man has been glorified, and God has been glorified in him. If God has been glorified in him, God will also glorify him in himself and will glorify him at once' (Jn 13:31-32).

This is the glorification that Jesus requests for both himself and his Father, in the priestly prayer: 'Glorify your Son so that the Son may glorify you' (Jn 17:1). He even repeats it: 'Glorify me in your own presence with the glory that I had in your presence before the world existed' (Jn 17:5). Here, Jesus is pleading for his own glorification in his passion-resurrection and the glorification of the Father in Jesus himself. As we shall now see, it is not a prayer asking to be saved from death – in the sense of being spared from it – as Jesus prayed in the other gospels. It is a prayer for his sacrificial transformation through the glorification of his passion, death and resurrection.

A prayer for the resurrection

In John's equivalent of the Gethsemane prayer, Jesus cries, 'Save me from this hour' (Jn 12:27). These words are often taken to mean that Jesus prays here to be spared the anguish and ordeal of his passion-death. If that were so, Jesus would then be praying for deliverance *from* death, which would give us an exact parallel to this Gethsemane prayer in the other gospels: 'that, if it were possible, the hour might pass from him' (Mk 14:35; cf Mt 26:39; Lk 22:42). But the same word of Jesus in the Greek (*ek*) can also be understood in a different way, to mean: 'Father, save me *out of* this hour.' This would not, then, be a prayer directly for deliverance from death, but a request of Jesus that his Father might bring him safely *through* his hour – 'out of' his struggle, anguish and death by means of the resurrection into glory.[10]

The Letter to the Hebrews seems to understand the Gethsemane prayer of Jesus in the same way: 'In the days of his flesh, Jesus offered up prayers and supplications, with loud cries and tears, to the one who was able to save him from death, and he was heard because of his reverent submission' (Heb 5:7). Jesus' prayer, this letter tells us, was heard. And yet, as we know, he was not saved from death but out of death – by his resurrection into glory. The Jerusalem Bible renders it accurately: 'The one who had the power to save him out of death' (Heb 5:7). Jesus prays for his glorification, his transfiguration and his transform-

---

10. Stanley writes: 'Consequently, it seems more plausible to understand that Jesus is represented here as petitioning the Father to bring him to salvation out of his hour, *not* to deliver him from the hour.' In his *Jesus in Gethsemane, op. cit.*, p 241; cf pp 101-2 (on Hebrews 5:7-10). See also *The New Jerusalem Bible, Standard Edition* (re Hebrews 5:7): 'Not saved from dying, since that was the whole purpose of his life, Jn 12:27 seq, but rescued from death after dying, Acts 2:24 seq. God transformed his death by raising him to glory after it.'

ation through his resurrection out of death and into glory. It is the same petition in the priestly prayer of Jesus: 'Father ... glorify your Son' (Jn 17:1; cf 17:5).

A gospel in prayer form

The whole priestly prayer is contained in embryo in a few introductory verses. They provide us with a beautiful example of the workings of John's mind. As we shall see in the next chapter, the evangelist winds his way into his subject like a tidal wave. He introduces his theme, then expands on it, and finally returns to it again in a spiral movement so as to develop and draw out the implications more fully. The mention of the 'glorification' of Jesus at the beginning of the priestly prayer (Jn 17:1), and again a few lines later (Jn 17:5), provides a kind of bracket or framework (technically an 'inclusion') which binds the first few verses of the prayer (Jn 17:1-5) into a closely knit unit by way of introduction to the prayer's subsequent development.

At the heart of this same passage, Jesus expands on the implications of his glorification for believers: 'to give eternal life to all whom you [Father] have given [me]' (Jn 17:2). He further explains the meaning of this life: 'And this is eternal life, that they may know you, the only true God, and Jesus Christ whom you have sent' (Jn 17:3). To 'know' is used here in the biblical sense of experiencing, and even more so in the Johannine sense of a progressive and ever-deepening penetration of the truth of Jesus by faith (cf Jn 8:31-32).

The priestly prayer is the prayer of Jesus for the glorification of his Father through the glorification of the Son in his passion-resurrection, and for the gift of eternal life to believers through their coming to know Jesus; for this is the whole purpose of John's gospel: 'That you may come to believe that Jesus is the Messiah, the Son of God, and that through believing you may have life in his name' (Jn 20:31). The central insight of John – Jesus as the revelation, in person, of the Father – is expanded beautifully in this prayer, where it is supported with a rich variety of typical Johannine terms that can be found throughout the fourth gospel. The priestly prayer of Jesus is a synthesis of the evangelist's whole teaching. It is the entire gospel of John in prayer form, and the most developed insight into praying with the mind of Jesus himself.[11]

---

11. It is no coincidence that the great Carmelite saints highlight the priestly prayer of Jesus which expresses for them the pinnacle of Christian prayer. See the references to Teresa of Avila, John of the Cross, Elizabeth of the Trinity, Thérèse of Lisieux and Edith Stein in James McCaffrey OCD, *Captive Flames: A Biblical Reading of the Carmelite Saints*, Dublin: Veritas, 2005, section 'Carmel and the priestly prayer', pp 150-3; also pp 149-50.

For Pondering and Prayer

1. The central insight of John is that Jesus is the revelation in person of the Father (Jn 1:14; 14:6). How is this borne out in the great priestly prayer of Jesus?

2. John, unlike the other evangelists, never speaks explicitly of the solitary prayer of Jesus. Is this a lack? Or does he, in his treatment of Jesus at prayer, give us something that could be seen as lacking in the other gospels?

3. The priestly prayer of Jesus is an example of how 'the true worshippers will worship the Father in spirit and truth' (Jn 4:23). How can this be true when the priestly prayer contains no explicit reference to the Spirit?

A GUIDED *LECTIO DIVINA*

Jesus our friend (Jn 15:12-17)
This is my commandment, that you love one another as I have loved you. No one has greater love than this, to lay down one's life for one's friends. You are my friends if you do what I command you. I do not call you servants any longer, because the servant does not know what the master is doing; but I have called you friends, because I have made known to you everything that I have heard from my Father. You did not choose me but I chose you. And I appointed you to go and bear fruit, fruit that will last, so that the Father will give you whatever you ask him in my name. I am giving you these commands so that you may love one another.

Reading
Relax. Invoke the Holy Spirit. Then read this passage slowly, attentively and reverently, with mind and heart open to receive the word, ready to respond to whatever it asks of you. Know that it is a word of love from God addressed to you personally. Reread it two or three times – calmly, quietly and without haste.

Meditation

Make a mental note of a word or phrase that grips you in this passage. For example: 'You are my friends.' Think of someone whom you can truly call your 'friend'. What is it about them that makes you treasure them as a friend? What does their friendship tell you about Jesus as a friend? And what does friendship with Jesus tell you about how to be a friend to others?

Jesus speaks here of only one commandment: 'my commandment'. Recall another time that Jesus speaks of this commandment. For example: 'I give you a new commandment, that you love one another. Just as I have loved you, you also should love one another' (Jn 13:34). Is Jesus making an impossible demand? If not, how does he make it possible?

Prayer

Jesus explains the measure of this love: 'No one has greater love than this, to lay down one's life for one's friends.' This points to the supreme expression of his love on the cross. We might share the thoughts of our hearts with him in this way: 'Jesus, you know how often I fail to love others. I am powerless to love them as you do, without your strength. Help me, Lord. I come to you with an open heart. Fill it with your love, so that I may pour it out on others and give myself to them in whatever way you wish.'

Contemplation

True friends do not need words to communicate their love. Be still in the presence of Jesus with your heart quietly resting in his love. He knows you through and through – your talents, your weakness, your neediness; your desire, perhaps still unknown to yourself, to love to your full capacity. The love of God is unconditional. Bask in it quietly. Let Jesus love in you those whom he asks you to love.

Action

We are ambassadors for Christ, sent to bring his love into the lives of others. Your acts of kindness may be the only 'page' of the gospels your neighbour will ever 'read' – perhaps just a smile, a kind word, a reassurance, a helping hand. Resolve in future to be kind and gracious to the person who irritates or annoys you. Determine to be a true friend to those you meet, even when it means speaking an unpopular truth – though always in love (cf Eph 4:15). The Lord's new commandment is possible if you let Jesus live in you and let him, in you, love others as he has loved you.

CHAPTER 5

Praying with the Holy Spirit

The general theme of this book is prayer in the gospels. But we also need to remember that the role of the Holy Spirit is fundamental to any understanding of the scriptures and the mystery of Christian prayer. At prayer, we would be powerless without the Spirit. As Paul reminds us: 'Likewise the Spirit helps us in our weakness; for we do not know how to pray as we ought, but that very Spirit intercedes with sighs too deep for words' (Rom 8:26). In this exploration of prayer in the gospels, then, it is helpful to conclude by considering some of the evangelists' insights into the role of the Spirit. We do well especially to reread the important and most relevant passages from John and to linger on the words that pertain directly to the Spirit's action.

The gospel of John contains not only rich texts on the Spirit, but the Paraclete passages themselves;[1] there is nothing comparable to them in any of the other gospels. The synoptics do, of course, refer to the Spirit, such as his role of speaking through the believer in times of trial (cf Mk 13:11; Mt 10:19-20; Lk 12:11-12). But it is only in John – the summit and climax of an extended gospel tradition on prayer – that we can enter most deeply into the profound riches of the mysterious workings of the Spirit. Little wonder that the fourth gospel has been called the spiritual gospel – a word which we should not think of solely in terms of 'spirituality' as such, but in relation to the Holy Spirit. In fact, the whole teaching of John's gospel is contained within a framework of Jesus' teaching on the Spirit (Jn 1:32-33; 20:22). Moreover, when we read this gospel in the light of the passion-

---

1. Jn 14:16-17, 25-26; 15:26-27; 16:7-11, 12-15. See also the chart under 'The Paraclete' below, as well as the full quotations in the Appendix, 'Gospel Prayer Texts'.

resurrection of Jesus, a still deeper spiritual sense unfolds: through the revealing action of the Spirit who, as Jesus says, 'will teach you everything, and remind you of all that I have said to you' (Jn 14:26; cf 2:22; 12:16).

Jesus: dwelling place of the Spirit

The Baptist introduces Jesus as the dwelling place of the Spirit: 'I saw the Spirit descending from heaven like a dove, and it remained on him' (Jn 1:32). Here, the word 'remain' (*menô*) takes on its full Johannine sense: it designates Jesus as a fixed, permanent dwelling place of the Spirit. The impact of this description of Jesus is further emphasised by the repetition of this term in the next verse: 'He on whom you see the Spirit descend and remain ...' (Jn 1:33).

The baptism of Jesus is a defining moment in John, as it is in the other gospels. The identity of Jesus is affirmed. Here, he is designated as 'the one who baptises with the Holy Spirit' (Jn 1:33). The fullness of the Spirit dwells in him: 'He whom God has sent speaks the words of God, for he gives the Spirit without measure' (Jn 3:34). In Jesus, we have the definitive outpouring of the Spirit for the end of time (cf Acts 2:17-21; Joel 2:28-32) and 'from his fullness we have all received' (Jn 1:16). In him, Paul tells us, 'all the fullness of God was pleased to dwell' (Col 1:19; cf 2:9). To enter the kingdom and become a disciple of Jesus is to receive this same Spirit in baptism, to be born again 'of water and Spirit' (Jn 3:5; cf 3:3) and to be led by this same Spirit: 'For all who are led by the Spirit of God are children of God' (Rom 8:14; cf Gal 4:6-7). It is hardly surprising, then, that the presentation of Jesus as the dwelling place of the Spirit is followed immediately by the call of the first disciples (Jn 1:35-39).

A new creation

Significantly, the Spirit descends on Jesus at his baptism like a 'dove', an image which evokes – and is meant to evoke – the renewal of creation in the story of Noah (Gen 8:6-12). The 'dove' finally returned to the ark 'and there in its beak was a freshly plucked olive leaf' (Gen: 8:11) – the sign of a renewed creation after the flood. One last time, Noah sent out the dove 'and it did not return to him any more' (Gen 8:12). In the gospel of John, the Spirit descended on Jesus 'like a dove, and it remained on him' (Jn 1:32; cf 1:33). This marks the beginning of a new creation. The image of a bird also evokes God's creation of his own people. There, 'in the wilderness, in a land not sown' (Jer 2:2), he formed a people for himself to be his own possession: 'As an eagle stirs up its nest, and hovers over its young; as it spreads its wings, takes them up, and bears them aloft on its pinions, the Lord alone guided [his people]' (Deut 32:11-12).

The image of a bird also evokes the dawn of creation, where the creative Spirit of God hovers over the waste and the darkness: 'Earth was still an empty waste, and darkness hung over the deep; but already, over the waters, stirred the breath of God' (Gen 1:2).[2] Our Western minds are attuned to thinking of creation as God making something out of nothing. And in one sense this is true, of course. We find this concept in the later books of the Bible and in John himself: 'All things came into being through him, and without him not one thing came into being' (Jn 1:3). But we can also learn much from the Semitic way of thinking which is quite different: the act of creation draws order out of chaos, beauty out of ugliness, light out of darkness, life out of death. God looked into an amorphous mass and breathed life into formless and messy clay, just as we see him stretch out his hand to touch Adam into life, in Michelangelo's vision of creation.

Our Maker is the supreme artist and 'we are [his] work of art' (Eph 2:10; JB). He acts in the chaos, confusion, mess and sinfulness of our lives and out of it creates something beautiful for himself. There is a story told in the life of Picasso, of how he was once dining in a Paris restaurant. The waiter recognised the great man himself and accidentally spilt a container of gravy on the tablecloth. He was just about to rush off and clean up the mess when Picasso stopped him. He looked at the mess and,

---

2. Knox translation.

with a flick of his finger, gave it a head, eyes, ears, mouth, body and tail; and he gave the world a work of art – a thing of beauty. In the messiness of our lives – those moments of darkness, confusion, bewilderment and uncertainty, as we struggle to pray – the creative Spirit is at work, shaping us into the likeness of his Son. 'We know that all things work together for good for those who love God,' Paul assures us (Rom 8:28). And Augustine does not hesitate to add: 'even sins'.[3]

Born of the Spirit

Soon after we begin John's gospel, we meet Nicodemus who 'came to Jesus by night' (Jn 3:2) – out of the darkness into the light. This is no mere coincidence. It reflects the dramatic qualities of the fourth gospel, the clash between light and darkness. All drama turns on conflict.

Nicodemus is well disposed. He acknowledges that Jesus is a teacher: 'Rabbi, we know that you are a teacher who has come from God' (Jn 3:2). Great teacher that he is, Jesus begins to open up the truth through a dialogue of question and answer. He speaks of a mysterious birth 'from above' or 'again' (Jn 3:3). Nicodemus misunderstands: 'How can anyone be born after having grown old?' (Jn 3:4). So, Jesus repeats his teaching and draws Nicodemus on to a deeper spiritual understanding, inviting him to penetrate more deeply into the mystery. Jesus is not talking about natural birth, but about spiritual birth: 'What is born of the flesh is flesh, and what is born of the Spirit is spirit' (Jn 3:6). This can be grasped only by faith at a deep spiritual level in the light of the passion-resurrection of Jesus and the gift of the Spirit.

We notice how subtly and gradually Jesus draws Nicodemus, and us with him, into the mystery. First, Jesus explains: 'Very truly, I tell you, no one can see the kingdom of God without

---

3. The famous text from St Augustine, in which he quotes Rom 8:28 and adds *etiam peccata* ('even sins'), appears to be *De Correptione et Gratia* cap. 9; PL 44.930. The French poet, Paul Claudel, loved these words of Augustine and made them central to his play, *The Satin Slipper*.

being born from above' (Jn 3:3); and then he repeats it but expands: 'Very truly, I tell you, no one can enter the kingdom of God without being born of water and Spirit' (Jn 3:5). This heavenly birth, or rebirth, is a new creation through the waters of baptism and the gift of the Spirit.

Entering the kingdom

We can draw out even further the implications of Jesus' teaching in this scene. The dynamic import of the revelation is striking. Jesus warns Nicodemus, and us with him: 'Do not be astonished that I said to you, "You must be born from above"' (Jn 3:7). The kingdom in John is not something static, as we might speak of the United Kingdom, a place with fixed geographical limits. The kingdom of God cannot be understood in purely spatial terms. We capture the meaning more accurately if we render it as 'reign' or 'rule'. It is an active concept. Where God rules and reigns, there is the kingdom. It is a much broader concept even than 'church'. The church is at the service of the kingdom; it is commissioned to spread the reign of God.[4]

We notice the parallel between 'see' (Jn 3:3) and 'enter' the kingdom (Jn 3:5). 'To see', in John, speaks of vision with the eyes of faith. In fact, the evangelist never uses the simple noun 'faith' or 'belief'. He always uses the verb 'believe', which has a profound dynamic import. Nor does he ever use the phrase 'believe in'; it is always 'believe into' (*pisteuô eis*). It designates movement, a kind of voyage into the unknown, like the journey of Abraham who risked everything on the truth of God's word (Gen 12:1ff). It means to come under the influence, power, rule or reign of God. In a word, to allow God to take over or take possession of us (cf Phil 3:12). We ourselves have the ability or power to enter the kingdom, but only in submission to the action of the Spirit as he gradually takes over ever more fully in our lives. It is to grow in self-knowledge, becoming increasingly aware of our own powerlessness, weakness and frailty, and our utter dependence on God. It is, at the same time, to advance in

4. See *Lumen Gentium (Dogmatic Constitution on the Church)* 5.

prayer. We must allow the Spirit to take over, and we must surrender ever more fully to God's action. As we read, immediately
after this encounter with Nicodemus: 'He must increase, but I
must decrease' (Jn 3:30).

A prayer dialogue

We next hear of the Spirit, in John, when Jesus meets the Samaritan
woman by Jacob's well (Jn 4:7ff). Again, we find the Johannine
technique of dialogue: question, answer, and failure to understand. This encounter with Jesus is a close one-to-one exchange,
like a prayer scene. Jesus takes the initiative: 'Give me a drink' (Jn
4:7). He reveals himself here as eminently human, vulnerable,
needy. Disclosure begets disclosure. The woman is drawn to him
in his weakness, because he first shows his need of her.[5]

At first, there is misunderstanding: the thoughts of the
Samaritan woman are earthbound. She is thinking of the flowing spring water in the well. Then Jesus draws her on to a deeper
spiritual level of understanding and speaks of 'living water' (Jn
4:10). Not just flowing water, but water that gives life. The
woman is puzzled. 'Where do you get that living water?' she
asks. 'Are you greater than our ancestor Jacob, who gave us the
well?' (Jn 4:11-12). A beautiful example of Johannine irony! He
is! Just as he is greater than Abraham (cf Jn 8:53, 56). And so the
mystery gradually unfolds. A deep truth is beginning to dawn
on the woman. Jesus draws her on to an ever-deeper level of understanding: 'Everyone who drinks of this water will be thirsty
again, but those who drink of the water that I will give them will
never be thirsty' (Jn 4:13-14). This 'living water' will satisfy the
deepest longings of the woman's heart; it will slake the thirst of
every restless human heart. Moreover, it will become in her, and
in all believers, 'a spring of water gushing up to eternal life' (Jn
4:14). Prayer releases this inner spring of new life, welling up
within us and finding its fullness in the eternal life of God.

---

5. See the discussion of this episode in James McCaffrey, *A Biblical
Prayer Journey, op. cit.*, pp 230-71; see also St Augustine, in *Divine Office*,
vol II, pp 146-8.

The woman is captivated: 'Give me this water,' she says to Jesus (Jn 4:15), so reversing the opening of the scene when it was Jesus who asked her for a drink. Already she is open to the truth. Jesus now challenges her to face the truth about herself. 'Go, call your husband,' he says to her (Jn 4:16). She never flinches. She accepts the truth. She answers honestly, 'I have no husband' (Jn 4:17). Jesus replies, 'You have had five husbands, and the one you have now is not your husband. What you have said is true!' (Jn 4:18). She has never really been loved. Now, the truth has set her free (cf Jn 8:32). Her meeting with Jesus opens her up to the truth about herself – her weakness, her sinfulness – and the truth about Jesus: 'Sir,' she says, 'I see that you are a prophet' (Jn 4:19). Her entrance into the truth continues as she finally mentions the 'Messiah'. Then the whole truth unfolds: Jesus says to her, 'I am he, the one who is speaking to you' (Jn 4:26). The scene reaches its climax with the act of faith on the lips of the woman's towns-people: 'This is truly the Saviour of the world' (Jn 4:42). Here we have the pattern of all true prayer: a growing self-knowledge and an ever-deeper understanding of the mystery of God re-vealed in the person of Jesus.

'In spirit and truth'

But there is more to this scene, an even deeper disclosure. The woman introduces the theme of worship: 'Our ancestors wor-shipped on this mountain,' she says – and we can picture Mount Gerizim soaring in the background – 'but you say that the place where people must worship is in Jerusalem' (Jn 4:20). Worship cannot be confined to any particular place, even Jerusalem. So, Jesus draws the woman away from her earth-bound way of un-derstanding. He speaks of a *spiritual* 'place' of worship: 'in spirit and truth' (Jn 4:23-24; cf v. 20). 'The hour is coming, and is now here,' Jesus tells her, 'when the true worshippers will worship the Father in spirit and truth … God is spirit, and those who worship him must worship in spirit and truth' (Jn 4:23-24).

In a real sense, Jesus himself is already the true place of wor-ship 'in spirit and truth'. The Spirit had descended on Jesus at his baptism 'and it remained on him' (Jn 1:32; cf 1:33). Moreover, Jesus is the truth in person, 'full of grace and truth' (Jn 1:14; cf 14:6). In this sense, the 'hour' has already come. However, access to this place of worship 'in spirit and truth' was still closed to all worshippers, awaiting the gift of the Holy Spirit through the passion-resurrection of Jesus. Then the 'hour' would finally come for all believers to worship the Father 'in spirit and truth', at one with Jesus in the new temple of his glorified body (cf Jn 2:21; 1:14). This is the true nature of all Christian prayer: it is worship, in union with Jesus, under the action of the Spirit.

'Out of his heart'

John takes up the theme of 'living water' again at the centre of his gospel, where he explicitly identifies it as the Spirit. The occasion is the celebration of tabernacles, a harvest feast full of the symbolism of water and light. Jesus cries out: 'Let anyone who is thirsty come to me' (Jn 7:37). This is an echo of his words in Matthew: 'Come to me, all you that are weary and are carrying heavy burdens, and I will give you rest' (Mt 11:28). We are always seeking, consciously or unconsciously, for a still-point in an ever-changing world, and Jesus is the only one who can ultimately slake the deepest thirst of our restless human hearts. He is the centre of all Christian prayer and the only 'way' into the mystery of God (cf Jn 14:6; Heb 1:2). To take our eyes away from his sacred humanity, on the prayer journey, is to court disaster. The Letter to the Hebrews expresses it well: 'Let us run with perseverance the race that is set before us, looking to Jesus the pioneer and perfecter of our faith' (Heb 12:1-2).

The psalms give immortal and prayerful expression to these yearnings and longings of the heart, thirsting 'like the deer that yearns for running streams … like a dry, weary land without water' (Ps 41:2; 62:2; cf 83). 'Out of his heart shall flow rivers of living water' (Jn 7:38; RSV), we are told – that is, out of the heart of Jesus.[6] He is the source of the Spirit. John stresses the lavish

---

6. Not out of the heart of *the believer*, as we find in some translations: for example, 'out of the believer's heart' (NRSV).

outpouring of the Spirit, and these waters of salvation abound for all to drink. The evangelist repeats the lesson of this over-flowing gift of salvation in many ways: twenty or thirty gallons of wine at Cana (cf Jn 2:6), twelve baskets full of pieces remaining from the five barley loaves by the lakeside (cf Jn 6:13), a hundred and fifty-three fishes in one catch after toiling all night in vain (cf Jn 21:11). And now, we are told, the 'living water' of salvation will flow in torrents from the heart of Jesus (Jn 7:38; cf 19:34).

A new temple

All this is to fulfil the scriptures, or more precisely 'the scripture' (cf Jn 7:38; 19:28). It is a feature of the fourth gospel to evoke the scriptures in this way – anonymously, as it were. When John cites 'the scripture' as saying that living water shall flow from the heart of Jesus (cf Jn 7:38), he has in mind not just one biblical reference but a compilation of them. Several texts come readily to mind. At God's command, Moses struck water from the rock during the exodus: 'Strike the rock, and water will come out of it, so that the people may drink' (Ex 17:6). This water-from-the-rock theme pervades the Old Testament,[7] and Paul clearly ident-ifies the rock with Christ (1 Cor 10:4). This is all in harmony with John's preference for exodus symbolism – the paschal lamb (Jn 1:29), the bronze serpent (Jn 3:14), the crossing of the Red Sea (Jn 6:16-21), the manna (Jn 6:31-32) and the pillar of fire (Jn 8:12). Yet more significant still than these references, perhaps, with refer-ence to John's words on 'living water', is the image of the waters flowing in torrents from the side of the temple, in Ezekiel's vision of salvation at the end of time (Ez 47:1-12; cf Zech 14:8: Rev 22:1-2). Again, this symbolism harmonises beautifully with John's presentation of the risen Jesus as the new temple (Jn 2:21; cf 1:14; 4:23-24; 10:22-39; 11:47-53), the place of true prayer and worship 'in spirit and truth' (Jn 4:23-24).

John points us forward here to the passion-resurrection of Jesus as the condition for the torrential outpouring of the 'living

---

7. See, for example, Deut 8:15; Is 48:21; Ps 77:15-16; 113[A]:8; cf Is 44:3; 55:1; 58:11.

water', which is the Spirit: 'As yet there was no Spirit, because Jesus was not yet glorified' (Jn 7:39). Passion and resurrection are inseparably linked in the fourth gospel. They are both complementary facets of the 'glorification' of Jesus – his 'hour', one great paschal mystery: 'The hour has come for the Son of Man to be glorified … the hour has come; glorify your Son' (Jn 12:23; 17:1). This gift of the Spirit by the glorified Jesus is promised to believers: 'Now he said this about the Spirit, which believers in him were to receive' (Jn 7:39). Again, we note the dynamic thrust of faith in John. The disciple who will receive the Spirit is 'the one who believes in me' (Jn 7:38), that is, believes 'into' Jesus. It is on this ever-deepening journey of faith, into the one who is the 'Truth', that the believer will be led 'in spirit and truth'. Faith is an absolute condition for receiving that Spirit in prayer.

'His heart an open wound with love'[8]
John's reference to the glorified Jesus points us forward to Calvary. Here, there is a subtle echo of the scene with the Samaritan woman: Jesus first asking for water and then giving her the water of life. On the cross, the pattern is repeated. Jesus 'said (in order to fulfil the scripture), "I am thirsty"' (Jn 19:28). Again, not the scriptures, but the scripture: the whole loving plan of redemption revealed in all of the scriptures is fulfilled in the thirst of Jesus, his passionate longing to accomplish God's saving will. We look, now, to the pierced side of the crucified Saviour. Again, we find the symbol of water: 'One of the soldiers pierced his side with a spear, and at once blood and water came out' (Jn 19:34). Here, the promise of Jesus that out of his heart would flow 'rivers of living water' is fulfilled (cf Jn 7:38). In the earlier scene, at the feast of tabernacles, the water symbol had been identified as the Holy Spirit. Now, on Calvary, there is no explanation as such, but the context is eloquent. John brings out the deeper meaning of the death of Jesus with his own original slant: 'Then he bowed his head and gave up his spirit' (Jn 19:30);

---

8. This title is taken from the refrain of a poem by John of the Cross (*P* 7): *El Pastorcico* ('The Little Shepherd Boy').

literally, he 'handed over the Spirit'. There is no reference to 'handing over the Spirit' in any of the other gospels, where the description of Jesus' death is quite different, stating simply that he 'breathed his last' (Mk 15:37; Mt 27:50; Lk 23:46). John even seems to have inverted the natural order of the event. He mentions the 'handing over of the Spirit' after Jesus had already bowed his head in death. By mentioning the gift of the Spirit last, he highlights the special significance of the Spirit at the death of Jesus.

The context helps us to open up further the profound spiritual import of Jesus' death for a better grasp of the Spirit's role: 'When Jesus knew that all was now finished, he said (in order to fulfil the scripture), "I am thirsty"' (Jn 19:28). All was now finished. And this is emphasised by repetition when Jesus then cries out, 'It is finished' (Jn 19: 30). The original word, 'tetelestai', meaning 'It is finished', links back with the opening words of Jesus at the last supper: 'Having loved his own who were in the world, he loved them to the end' (Jn 13:1) – 'to the end' is, in Greek, 'eis telos', from which 'tetelestai' derives. The phrase, 'It is finished', speaks of love, the perfect, complete expression of love. When, on the cross, Jesus 'handed over' the Spirit, he released the full potential of love that had been pent up in his heart.

Also woven into this scene is an intimation of prayer. 'They will look on the one whom they have pierced' (Jn 19:37), writes John as his final comment on the death of Jesus. These words are in fact drawn directly from Zechariah and evoke the words immediately linked to them in the same verse of this prophecy: 'I will pour out a spirit of compassion and supplication on the house of David and the inhabitants of Jerusalem' (Zech 12:10) – or, as we read in the liturgy: 'I will pour out a spirit of kindness and prayer.' In this subtle way, the evangelist links the Saviour's very wounds with prayer and compassion. This profound mystery of the passion is a perennial object of prayer for all who walk the contemplative way. In communion with the crucified Jesus, we can learn the lesson of compassion when we 'look on

the one whom they have pierced' (Jn 19:37); 'by his wounds,'
Peter tells us, 'you have been healed' (1 Pet 2:24). God enters
through our wounds: it is those unhealed, everlasting wounds
of Jesus that heal our broken world.

Diptych of the paschal mystery

In John, the passion and resurrection of Jesus are like two sides
of a diptych. Together they form a single unified whole. The
evangelist refers to them as the 'exaltation' or the 'lifting up' (cf
Jn 3:14; 8:28; 12:32), the 'glorification' and the 'hour' of Jesus (Jn
12:28; 17:1, 5). John is clearly underlining an important link between these two complementary facets of the paschal mystery.
The risen Jesus appeared to his disciples and 'he showed them
his hands and his side' (Jn 20:20). Moreover, the evangelist is
careful to link this gesture with the gift of the Spirit: 'He breathed
on them and said to them, "Receive the Holy Spirit"' (Jn 20:22).
In Luke, the risen Jesus also pointed to the wounds of his passion, 'his hands and his feet' (Lk 24:40). The purpose of the gesture is the same in both gospels: to identify the risen Jesus with
the Saviour on the cross.

John, however, is the only evangelist who mentions the 'side'
of Jesus. This not only identifies the risen Jesus with the one who
suffered and died. It also links this whole scene back to the
piercing of Jesus, the 'water' issuing from his side (Jn 19:34) and
the 'handing over of the Spirit' (cf Jn 19:30) on the cross. This
passion scene, in turn, is the fulfilment of Jesus' promise at the
feast of tabernacles that out of his heart would flow 'rivers of living water', which, as we have seen, John identifies as the Spirit
(Jn 7:38-39). And so, the final gift of the Spirit by the risen Jesus is
like a climax to John's teaching on the mystery of the Spirit.

A Spirit-filled community

The gift of the risen Jesus to his disciples reveals a fruit of the
Spirit's action: peace (cf Gal 5:22). Jesus said to them, 'Peace be
with you' (Jn 20:19). He even repeated the words a second time
(Jn 20:21) as 'he showed them his hands and his side' (Jn 20:20) –

the scars of his passion and death. The link between this gesture of Jesus and his gift of peace helps to clarify the meaning of true peace. Peace is often mentioned in the other gospels. At the birth of Christ, it was God's first gift to the world: 'Peace among those whom he favours' (Lk 2:14). Then, just before his death, Jesus says to his disciples at the last supper: 'Peace I leave with you; my peace I give to you. I do not give to you as the world gives. Do not let your hearts be troubled, and do not let them be afraid' (Jn 14:27). This peace is pure gift, the peace of Jesus himself – 'my' peace, he says, a peace that the world cannot give. It dispels fear. But it is something even deeper still. It is peace in union with Jesus: 'I have said this to you, so that in me you may have peace' (Jn 16:33).

Only when we are at one with the crucified-risen Jesus can we find true Christian peace. It is a dying with the crucified Saviour to our own selfishness and an entering with the glorified Jesus into the joy of the resurrection: 'The disciples,' we are told, 'rejoiced when they saw the Lord' (Jn 20:20). This change within them – the transformation of their fear into peace and joy – is the fruit of the Spirit's action in them. It is also an authentic sign of the Spirit at work deep in the heart of everyone who prays. It has nothing to do with the transient satisfaction and contentment of self-indulgence; rather, it is a peace and joy in the Spirit born of intimacy with a crucified-risen Saviour.

In the power of the Spirit
After his resurrection, Jesus gives the Holy Spirit to his disciples (cf Jn 20:22). This final mention of the Spirit in John forms a kind of bracket (technically known as an 'inclusion') with his first reference to the Spirit (Jn 1:32-33) – thus enclosing the whole gospel within the framework of the action of the Holy Spirit. In that opening chapter, the Spirit descended on Jesus at his baptism. There, we met a Jesus who was the permanent dwelling place of the Spirit and the inaugurator of a new creation. He was also the one who would make disciples 'with the Holy Spirit' (Jn 1:33; cf 3:5). Now, after his death, this is what he does: the risen Jesus

'breathed' on the first disciples (Jn 20:22). The gesture – like that of the 'dove' at the baptism – evokes the dawn of the first creation. God 'formed man ... and breathed into his nostrils the breath of life' (Gen 2:7). But even more significant for an understanding of this 'breathing' of the Spirit is Ezekiel's vision of the valley of the dry bones (Ezek 37:1-14). At the Lord's command, the breath came into the bones 'and they lived, and stood on their feet, a vast multitude' (Ezek 37:10). Then the Lord explained the 'breathing' to the prophet: 'these bones are the whole house of Israel' (Ezek 37:11).

Here we have the promise of a new people of God: 'I will put my spirit within you, and you shall live' (Ezek 37:14). We know from the Acts of the Apostles how the terrified disciples in the upper room were transformed at Pentecost into fearless witnesses to the resurrection by the power of the Spirit (Acts 2:1ff). In anticipation of that event, the risen Jesus now launches the church, the new community of believers, on its saving mission to the world: '"As the Father has sent me, so I send you." When he had said this, he breathed on them and said to them, "Receive the Holy Spirit. If you forgive the sins of any, they are forgiven"' (Jn 20:21-23). Prayer finds its place at the heart of this saving mission of the church. It helps to make all those who pray into more fitting instruments of the Spirit. Ultimately, all prayer is at the service of the church.

The Paraclete

The Paraclete passages in John help us to understand more fully the mystery of the Spirit's action in prayer.[9] Translations often give 'Advocate' or 'Counsellor', though the word used in the original is actually *Paraklêtos*:[10] it derives from *para*, meaning

9. For an excellent treatment of the Paraclete passages in John, see Ignace de La Potterie SJ & Stanislaus Lyonnet SJ, *The Christian Lives by the Spirit*, New York: Alba House, 1971, chap 3, 'The Paraclete', pp 57-77.

10. In the quotations, I will use the term 'Paraclete' throughout, as a literal translation of the original Greek, rather than use the variations found in other translations.

'alongside', and *kaleô*, 'call'. It refers to the one who is summoned and stands beside us, coming to our aid as an assistant, a defender, an advocate – one who pleads on our behalf. Outside the fourth gospel, it is used only once in the New Testament, where it designates Jesus in glory: 'We have an advocate with the Father, Jesus Christ the righteous; and he is the atoning sacrifice for our sins' (1 Jn 2:1-2).

The Book of Revelation takes up and develops this theme. There we see 'the slain Lamb' standing before the throne as 'advocate' or 'intercessor' (Rev 5:6, 9, 12; 13:8). So, too, does the Letter to the Hebrews (Heb 7:23-27; 8:1; 9:11-12). All the work of 'expiation' on earth becomes in heaven like a great prayer of intercession to the Father by Jesus now in glory. The praying community prays at one with this powerful and eternal prayer of the risen Jesus. 'In the earthly liturgy, by way of foretaste,' Vatican II tells us, 'we share in that heavenly liturgy which is celebrated in the holy city of Jerusalem toward which we journey as pilgrims, and in which Christ is sitting at the right hand of God, a minister of the sanctuary and of the true tabernacle'.[11]

In the fourth gospel, John gives a special role to the Paraclete, not primarily as advocate, or intercessor, but as teacher and as witness. The arrangement of the five passages on the Spirit is significant. We can show it schematically as follows:

1st passage (Jn 14:16-17) Introduction to the Paraclete
2nd passage (Jn 14:25-26) Paraclete as *teacher*
3rd passage (Jn 15:26-27) Paraclete as *witness*
4th passage (Jn 16:7-11) Paraclete as *witness*
5th passage (Jn 16:12-15) Paraclete as *teacher*

The evangelist introduces the Paraclete in the first passage and develops his role as 'teacher' in the second. He then moves away from the Spirit's role as 'teacher' and introduces the Paraclete as 'witness' in the third, expanding on it in the fourth. Finally, he returns to the original theme of 'teacher' in the fifth

---

11. *Sacrosanctum Concilium (Constitution on the Sacred Liturgy)* 8; this passage makes reference to Rev 21:2; Col 3:1; Heb 8:2.

and final passage, linking it back to the same theme of 'teacher' in the second. This is an example of how John presents his teaching in a cyclic movement, which is characteristic of his style throughout the gospel. In this way, he draws us with him as he winds his way in a spiral movement and penetrates, like a tidal wave, ever more deeply into the riches of God's word. To read and ponder the word of God prayerfully with the beloved disciple is to return to it again and again, and to enter ever more deeply into a world of mystery that only gradually unfolds to faith in the person of Jesus.

'The Lord is the Spirit'

At first sight, this profound and extensive teaching on the Paraclete may appear strange. As we have already observed, John's is the last gospel, written some sixty years or more after the death of Jesus. Almost half a century of church history had passed since then, and the first believers were still waiting expectantly for the Lord's imminent return (cf 2 Thess 2:1-2). But Jesus had not yet returned. Moreover, the last of the disciples would soon be dead, and the link with the Jesus of history would then – apparently – be severed irreparably. So, the church had the problem of how to preserve the unity and purity of Jesus' teaching untarnished and pass it on faithfully to the future generations of believers. These were the concrete circumstances of the early church in which the teaching on the Paraclete developed under the Spirit's action. Jesus would come again at the end of time (Rev 22:7, 12, 20; 1 Cor 16:22), but he would also return in the immediate future. This does not mean just in the apparitions of the risen Jesus (Jn 14:18). Even more than this: he would come again and be present in the church until the end of time, through the presence and working of the Spirit (cf Jn 14:16; Mt 28:20). In this way, the bond with the historical Jesus would be preserved intact and the teaching of Jesus in his ministry maintained in its unity and depth, within the Spirit-filled community of the church.

In John Masefield's play, *The Trial of Jesus*, Procula, the wife of Pilate, asks Longinus, the centurion who stood at the foot of the cross, for news of Jesus: 'Do you think he is dead?' 'No, lady, I don't,' he replies. 'Then where is he?' she asks. And he answers: 'Let loose in the world.'[12] It is only through the Spirit that we can now meet the risen Jesus present in the praying church: no longer confined or conditioned by time and space. Little wonder Joan of Arc could say to her ecclesiastical accusers: 'For me, Christ and the church are one.' And Jesus reassures his disciples on the eve of his passion-death about his imminent departure: 'Nevertheless I tell you the truth: it is to your advantage that I go away, for if I do not go away, the Paraclete will not come to you; but if I go, I will send him to you' (Jn 16:7). It is this same Jesus, crucified and risen, whom we encounter and commune with in prayer through the Spirit. Indeed, it is he who now prays with us and in us – the same person who walked the roads of Judea and preached the word of God by the lakeside in Galilee.

A prayer for the Spirit
John introduces the first Paraclete passage with these words: 'I will ask the Father, and he will give you another Paraclete, to be with you forever' (Jn 14:16). This means that the coming of the Spirit will be a response to the prayer of Jesus. The priestly prayer of Jesus at the last supper (Jn 17) may also be seen as an extension of Jesus' prayer for the Spirit (cf Lk 11:13; Eph 3:14-21). For although it contains no explicit reference to the Spirit, the Paraclete passages and this prolonged intercessory prayer of Jesus in John are both deeply embedded in the extended discourses of Jesus at the last supper and inseparably linked there, as we have seen. Indeed, the priestly prayer of Jesus can be seen as the whole gospel of John in prayer form. And it is a prayer for all believers to be consecrated in truth (Jn 17:19) and to be the dwelling place of love (Jn 17:26) – both of which are the work of the Spirit.

We are told that the Spirit will be 'another Paraclete' (Jn

---

12. John Masefield, *The Trial of Jesus*, London: William Heinemann, 1925, pp 95-6.

14:16), implying that Jesus himself, too, is a Paraclete. So the Spirit will continue the work of Jesus among his disciples. Moreover, the Paraclete is 'the Spirit of truth' (Jn 14:17); his action is centred entirely on the person of Jesus who is the Truth (Jn 14:6; cf 1:14). The Spirit cannot be received by 'the world' (Jn 14:17). Here, Jesus means the world of 'darkness', of unbelief (cf Jn 1:10), which has deliberately closed its eyes to the light of Christ; it has not got the spiritual eye of faith.

The breath of the Spirit enters the human sanctuary like a breeze. It bursts open the inner window of the human heart in order to penetrate within. It is a pure gift of God. This opening is the effect of the Spirit's action, but it is also its condition: we need to open with faith to receive the Paraclete. The 'world' of unbelievers, however, is radically incapable of opening to the new spiritual presence of the Paraclete. The disciples, in contrast, open willingly to receive it in faith. Faith unlocks the human spirit to receive the secret riches of the Holy Spirit – a faith ever-searching in prayer for a deeper meaning and understanding of what is happening, here and now, in our lives; a faith that is seeking God. So we must come to prayer in a spirit of faith: 'I believe; help my unbelief' (Mk 9:24).

An indwelling presence of the Spirit

This first Paraclete passage shows John using a subtle variation of prepositions to describe three different kinds of presence by the Spirit. They indicate varying degrees of intimacy. Jesus assures his disciples that, at present, the Paraclete abides 'with' them, alongside them (*para*, Jn 14:17); that, in the future and for all time, he will be 'with' them (*meta*, Jn 14:16); and also 'in' them (*en*, Jn 14:17). The Spirit is already present 'with' them (*para*, Jn 14:17) during the ministry of Jesus: he is close to them or near them in the person of Jesus on whom the Spirit 'descends' and 'remains' at the outset of the gospel (Jn 1:32, 33; cf 3:34); the disciples perceive the Spirit's action already at work in Jesus, here and now, during his ministry. Jesus also promises another kind of presence of the Spirit for the future: 'He will be with you for-

ever' (*meta*, Jn 14:16). This is not the familiar presence of the
Spirit close to the disciples and present in Jesus throughout his
ministry. It indicates a presence of the Spirit who aids and as-
sists the church, as Jesus promised: 'I am with you always, to the
end of the age' (*meta*, Mt 28:20). But there is yet another new
kind of presence promised for the future: the Paraclete will be
'in' (*en*, Jn 14:17) the disciples. This will be a presence deep within
the heart of the believer – an indwelling presence (cf Jn 14:23;
Rom 5:5; 8:26-27). Jesus had already promised this inner presence of the Spirit to all believers after his glorification though his
passion-death (Jn 7:39). Unlike the world, the disciples are able
to 'see' (cf Jn 3:3; 7:39; 12:21) and 'know' the Spirit (cf Jn 8:31-32)
by faith, and – through seeing and knowing – to 'receive' him (Jn
14:17). We need to pray in faith: 'Come, Holy Spirit!'

This first Paraclete passage is John's introduction to the role
of the Spirit as our advocate and helper. So, understandably, it
does not tell us a great deal explicitly about the precise nature of
the Spirit's action. But it shows us that as 'another Paraclete', his
role will parallel that of Jesus himself who was, in some sense,
also a Paraclete. As 'the Spirit of truth', his action will focus entirely on Jesus, who *is* the Truth. His future spiritual presence
will be essentially an inner working in the hearts of those who
receive him in faith.

The promptings of the Spirit

Jesus himself was a teacher (Jn 3:2).[13] So, too, the Spirit is a
teacher. In the second Paraclete passage, Jesus explains how. He
begins with a distinction between his own teaching – 'I have said
these things to you' (Jn 14:25) – and the future teaching of the
Paraclete – 'But the Paraclete … will teach you everything' (Jn
14:26). Jesus is the Truth in person (cf Jn 14:6), the Word of God
enfleshed (cf Jn 1:14). In him, revelation is complete and definitive. But the word of Jesus must not become a dead letter. The
Spirit's teaching is indispensable, making the word of Jesus 'liv-

---

13. See also the following verses in John, where Jesus is referred to as
'teacher': Jn 1:38; 11:28; 13:13-14; 20:16.

ing and active, sharper than any two-edged sword, piercing until it divides soul from spirit, joints from marrow' (Heb 4:12). Jesus' word must be accepted and assimilated by faith. What Jesus taught must become an inner possession. John expresses this characteristically as to 'abide in the teaching of Christ' (2 Jn 1:9) and to abide in his word (cf Jn 8:31; 15:7). Jesus chides the sceptical: 'There is no place in you for my word' (Jn 8:37); 'You do not have [my] word abiding in you' (Jn 5:38). To make the words and actions of Jesus penetrate deeply into believing hearts at prayer is precisely the teaching role of the Holy Spirit. Jesus also refers to it as 'the anointing that … abides' in the believer by which we 'know the truth' (cf 1 Jn 2:27, 20-21).

Jesus goes on to designate this teaching of the Spirit more precisely as a 'recalling' or 'reminding': '[He will] remind you of all that I have said to you' (Jn 14:26). The Latin equivalent for 'recalling' is *recordare*. It captures precisely the nature of the Spirit's action: *re* – again; *cor* – heart; *dare* – to give. The Spirit communicates the word to the heart. It is not enough for the head to grasp and understand the word. The word must move under the action of the Spirit from the head to the heart – often a long, painful and challenging journey. Jerome, in his Latin version of the Bible known as the Vulgate, uses the term *suggerô* to translate this 'recalling' action of the Spirit (Jn 14:26). It captures beautifully the delicate action of the Spirit in prayer. He teaches by suggesting. 'Do not grieve the Holy Spirit of God,' we read in the Letter to the Ephesians (4:30), by refusing to accept his inspirations. The Spirit invites a response. There is no constraint, no force, no compulsion. He draws us gently, quietly, with noiseless promptings in prayer – his suggestions urging us, as it were, to a free and open acceptance and surrender: to a *fiat*.

The memory of the church

But in John's gospel, the term 'recall' takes on a special significance. The action of 'recalling' is mentioned three times, apart from this second Paraclete passage (Jn 2:17, 22; 12:16). The first two examples are at the cleansing of the temple (Jn 2:13-22). The disciples, we are told, remembered the words of the psalm, 'Zeal for your house will consume me' (Jn 2:17; Ps 68:10). Jesus then proceeds to foretell the destruction of the temple: 'Destroy this temple, and in three days I will raise it up' (Jn 2:19). The evangelist explains that Jesus was speaking of the temple of his body, and comments, 'After [Jesus] was raised from the dead, his disciples remembered that he had said this; and they believed the scripture and the word that Jesus had spoken' (Jn 2:22). The third example of this act of recalling is mentioned in the response of the disciples when Jesus enters Jerusalem riding in triumph on a donkey. The event is the fulfilment of the words of Zechariah: 'Look, your king is coming, sitting on a donkey's colt' (Jn 12:15; Zech 9:9). The evangelist comments: 'His disciples did not understand these things at first; but when Jesus was glorified, then they remembered that these things had been written of him and had been done to him' (Jn 12:16).

Jesus and the Spirit cannot be separated in the work of teaching: the Spirit does not bring to mind a new revelation. But after the glorification of Jesus through his death-resurrection, the disciples, under the recalling action of the Spirit, experience the deeper spiritual significance of the event and the relevance of the scripture to what has happened. The Spirit will not just remind the disciples of a word or action of Jesus which they may have forgotten. The words and actions of Jesus can suddenly explode with new meaning, by the power of the Spirit, when they are relevant to something happening in our lives. The Spirit will re-present the Christ-event and make it present again spiritually by faith in the hearts of believers. This is how the Spirit works: we discover new insights and hidden mysterious meanings when we read the word of God with our own life-experiences exposed to the light of the Spirit. 'Let [the] heart at length be ploughed by some keen grief or deep anxiety,' wrote Newman, 'and scripture is *a new book*.'[14]

---

14. John Henry Newman, *An Essay in Aid of a Grammar of Assent*, Garden City, New York: Image Books, 1955, p 80; italics mine.

Furthermore, the Father will send the Spirit 'in [Jesus'] name' (Jn 14:26) – that is, in close communion with Jesus and revealing who Jesus really is. A name indicates the deepest reality of a person. 'I have come in my Father's name,' Jesus said (Jn 5:43). He lived his earthly life in close communion with his Father. He also said to him in prayer: 'I have made your name known' (Jn 17:6; cf 17:26). Jesus has revealed God as he really is in person: the Father of his Son. The Father and the Son will send the Spirit, in close and perfect communion with each other, to reveal Jesus precisely as he is in the deepest mystery of his being: the Son of God. He will stir up faith in the person of Jesus as the Father's only Son (cf Jn 1:14, 18), who is truly by nature the Son of God, his heavenly Father.

'Into all truth'

After the second Paraclete passage, the treatment of the Spirit as teacher is left suspended, as it were, still awaiting further development – apparently interrupted by the Spirit's role as witness in the third and fourth passages, as we shall see later. Only with the fifth Paraclete passage does the evangelist finally take up the teaching role of the Spirit again, developing it, deepening it and coming back full circle to this theme explored in the second passage. The fifth and final passage on the Spirit's teaching role begins with an apparent contradiction. Jesus had previously said to his disciples at the last supper: 'I have made known to you everything that I have heard from my Father' (Jn 15:15). Now he informs them: 'I still have many things to say to you' (Jn 16:12); then he adds significantly, 'but you cannot bear them now' (Jn 16:12). Here, the stress is on the 'now'. It offers a contrast between the present ministry of Jesus, the here and now when the disciples cannot yet fully grasp the teaching of Jesus, and a future time after the coming of the Spirit. Then the disciples will have a deeper understanding of the mystery of Jesus – his life, his actions, his words. As already emphasised, the Spirit will not provide a new doctrine. He will draw out the implications of what Jesus has taught his disciples and shed new light on it.

The Spirit will guide the disciples 'into all the truth' (Jn 16:13), leading them into a deeper understanding of the truth fully revealed in the person of Jesus (cf Jn 14:6; 1:14). This 'guiding' action of the Spirit is described literally, in the original, as 'to lead along the way' of all truth. The phrase evokes again the words of Jesus at the supper: 'I am the way, and the truth, and the life' (Jn 14:6). For the devout Israelite, this would recall the story of the exodus, the 'way' God led his people out of Egypt across the desert into the promised land (cf Deut 8:2). The Spirit will lead believers along the 'way' of the new 'departure' – literally, 'exodus' (cf Lk 9:31) – the 'passover' of Jesus to the Father though his passion-resurrection (cf Jn 13:1). This is the path of all true prayer: it plunges us ever more deeply into the paschal mystery – a dying to our own selfishness and a joyful experience of rising with Jesus.

The declaration of the Spirit

The Paraclete 'will not speak on his own'; literally, he will not speak 'from himself'. Instead, '[he] will speak whatever he hears' (Jn 16:13). Jesus says, and he repeats it: 'He will take what is mine' (Jn 16:14, 15). Jesus, too, has not spoken 'from himself' (cf Jn 7:17ff; 12:49; 14:10) but only 'as the Father instructed [him]' (Jn 8:28; cf 12:50). Or, as he says to his disciples: 'I have made known to you everything that I have heard from my Father' (Jn 15:15; cf 8:28; 12:50). This all means that the Spirit will speak what he has heard from Jesus, just as Jesus speaks what he himself has heard from his Father. Revelation is perfectly one. It takes its origin in the heart of the Trinity – from its source in the Father, manifested in the Son and completed in the Spirit: 'All that the Father has is mine. For this reason I said that [the Spirit] will take what is mine and declare it to you' (Jn 16:15). To be a true disciple is to be a listener: 'Everyone who belongs to the truth listens to my voice' (Jn 18:37). To pray as a disciple is also to listen: to enter into communion with an eternal listening within the inner life of God, praying like Mary of Bethany 'who sat at the Lord's feet and listened to what he was saying' (Lk 10:39).

The teaching role of the Spirit, in this fifth Paraclete passage, is described as 'to declare'. The term *anangellô* is here repeated three times (16:13-15). It does not refer to a public proclamation of the message, nor does it refer to a completely new revelation. It means to throw light on something hidden and mysterious, to clarify an obscure saying (cf Jn 16:25), explaining its deeper meaning. So, it is no coincidence that we find it in the Book of Daniel, in the sense of interpreting dreams and visions (Dan 2:2, 27; 5:15; 9:23). Revelation in John is not something inert or static. It is never merely about ideas. It is life-giving: 'The words that I have spoken to you are spirit and life' (Jn 6:63). It implies communication and enables the believer to penetrate into the inner life of God and to live in communion with the Father through the Son in the Spirit (cf Jn 4:23-24). Received in faith, revelation enables us to become 'participants of the divine nature' (2 Pet 1:4), sharing in an eternal exchange and dialogue of love: 'We declare to you what we have seen and heard so that you also may have fellowship with us; and truly our fellowship is with the Father and with his Son Jesus Christ' (1 Jn 1:3). It is the Spirit who quickens and activates that fellowship, releasing and enkindling the fire of God's eternal love within us when we pray.

The Paraclete will declare to believers 'the things that are to come' (*erchomena*, Jn 16:13). In the historical setting of the last supper, these are the events of the passion-resurrection of Jesus. They are repeatedly designated in John as the 'hour' of Jesus.[15] The Spirit will reveal this 'hour' – not just throwing light on it, manifesting it to the disciples, but also making it present in the church until the end of time. It is like a still-point in the vortex of salvation history: everything pivots around it – past, present and future. The Spirit will give believers an understanding of the whole new final order of redemption ushered in by this 'hour', the new dispensation of divine providence issuing from the passion-resurrection of Jesus – the 'eschatological age', as it is called, or the 'final days'. The Paraclete will disclose the meaning of history in the light of the life and teaching of Jesus, deep-

---

15. See Jn 2:4; 4:21, 23; 7:30; 8:20; 12:23, 27; 13:1; 16:2, 4, 32; 17:1.

ening, clarifying and developing it. He will show in all things the design of God's plan of redemption (Acts 20:27), shedding on every event, in every place and in every age, the radiant light of the truth revealed in Jesus. In this way, the Spirit will 'glorify' Jesus (Jn 16:14; cf 17:1-5) which, in John, is to release through the word the saving power of God's love revealed in Jesus: God is glorified when he shows mercy.

In a hostile world

John introduces the role of the Spirit as witness in the third Paraclete passage. We know that Jesus himself was a witness: 'For this I was born, and for this I came into the world, to testify to the truth' (Jn 18:37; cf 18:19-20). So, too, the Spirit will be a witness. This third Paraclete passage is explicit: 'He will testify on my behalf,' Jesus says (Jn 15:26). The immediate context helps to determine the precise nature of the Spirit's witness. Jesus has just spoken about the future hostility of the world – the hatred and persecution which his followers will have to endure as his disciples: 'If the world hates you, be aware that it hated me before it hated you ... "Servants are not greater than their master." If they persecuted me, they will persecute you ... "They hated me without a cause"' (Jn 15:18, 20, 25). Then he explains the need for the Paraclete's witness: 'I have said these things to you to keep you from stumbling' (Jn 16:1); literally, he says: 'to keep you from being scandalised', which in gospel terms means to lose faith in Jesus (cf Jn 6:61; Mk 6:3).

The witness of the Paraclete, then, will support the disciples in their trials of faith. As Jesus explains: 'They will put you out of the synagogues' (Jn 16:2); that is, his followers will be expelled from the community and even be put to death, ostensibly so as to be 'offering worship to God' (Jn 16:2). This witness of the Spirit, like his teaching, is directed not to the world, but to disciples: 'When the Paraclete comes,' Jesus says, 'whom I will send to you ...' (Jn 15:26). And: 'If I do not go away, the Paraclete will not come to you; but if I go, I will send him to you' (Jn 16:7). The Spirit will strengthen, support and encourage believers, as well as enlighten them when their faith and endurance are sternly put to the test. In the midst of hostility and adversity, the Paraclete will act secretly within the disciples and bear witness to Jesus as the truth – in opposition to the emptiness, falsity and pride of an unbelieving world that has deliberately rejected Jesus and is steeped in the darkness of its own sin: 'If I had not come and spoken to them, they would not have sin; but now they have no excuse for their sin' (Jn 15:22).

The inner witness of the Spirit

This same Paraclete passage draws attention explicitly to the witness of the disciples: 'You also are to testify' (Jn 15:27). The other gospels, likewise, speak of witness in a similar context of hostility: the world's hatred (Mt 24:9; cf Jn 15:18, 19, 23-25), persecution on account of Jesus (Mt 10:23; Lk 21:12; cf Jn 15:20), maltreatment in the synagogues (Mk 13:9; Lk 12:11; 21:12; cf Jn 16:2). These all form part of the challenge to future witness by the disciples in times of adversity and opposition. The Spirit will speak through them and in them (cf Mk 13:11; Mt 10:20). He will teach them what they should say (cf Lk 12:12) when they are 'dragged before governors and kings because of [Jesus], as a testimony to them and the Gentiles' (Mt 10:18). A modern 'witness', Whittaker Chambers, describes well this public testimony of a disciple: 'A witness, in the sense that I am using the word, is a man whose life and faith are so completely one that when the challenge comes to step out and testify for his faith, he does so, disregarding all risks, accepting all consequences.'[16]

It is only in John, however, that the Spirit himself is directly presented as a witness. The evangelist clearly distinguishes this inner witness of the Spirit and the external testimony of the disciples, however closely linked they may happen to be. Augustine expresses the difference well: 'Because the Spirit will bear witness, you also will bear witness; he in your hearts, you

---

16. From Whittaker Chambers, *Witness*, New York: Random House, 1952, p 5.

with your voices; he by inspiring, you by speaking aloud.'[17] There will be moments of doubt and discouragement in prayer, dangers of scandals, temptations to abandon the struggle, times when nothing seems to happen and when there are only distractions, confusion, emptiness and dryness of spirit. Then the Spirit as witness will act as Defender of Jesus within us, strengthening us in our faith so that we will be able to bear public witness to the truth we have assimilated in moments of quiet communion with God. As Paul expresses it so well: 'My grace is sufficient for you, for power is made perfect in weakness ... for whenever I am weak, then I am strong' (2 Cor 12:9, 10).

The challenge of the light

In the fourth Paraclete passage, John develops the role of the Spirit as witness: 'He will prove the world wrong about sin and righteousness and judgement' (Jn 16:8). The standard translations do not quite capture the meaning of the Greek original, neither the *NRSV* as here, nor other major editions of the Bible: the *RSV*, for example, reads: 'He will convince the world ...' while the *NJB* has: 'He will show the world how wrong it was'. The original term is *elenchô*. It is found only twice elsewhere in the fourth gospel (cf Jn 3:20; 8:46), and it designates to 'expose', 'bring to light' or 'reveal'. Jesus says, when speaking to Nicodemus: 'For all who do evil hate the light and do not come to the light, so that their deeds may not be exposed' (*elenchthê*, Jn 3:20). In the verse that immediately follows, it is used in exact parallel with the term *phaneróô*, which means to 'expose', 'manifest' or 'make clear': 'But those who do what is true come to the light, so that it may be clearly seen (*phanerôthê*) that their deeds have been done in God' (Jn 3:21).

So, in John's final treatment of the Paraclete as witness, we are actually told that the Spirit will bring to light the world's sin, righteousness and judgement. There is no question here of the Spirit convincing or converting the world. The witness of the Spirit is not directed to the world, for in this context the world is

---

17. See St Augustine, *In Joann.*, Tract. 93, 1: PL 35, 1864.

still the sphere of darkness and 'cannot receive' the Spirit, 'because it neither sees him nor knows him' (Jn 14:17). As we have seen, the Spirit works secretly in the heart of the believer. It is there that he will reveal the truth about everything, showing sin, righteousness and judgement for what they really are.

Sinning against the light

The Paraclete will expose to believers the truth about sin as unbelief because, in the words of Jesus, those who are of the world 'do not believe in me' (Jn 16:9). This statement is emphatic: they refuse to believe in Jesus – a free, deliberate choice (cf Jn 14:17). Just as all the commandments can, in John, be reduced to one – 'a new commandment' (Jn 13:34), 'my commandment' (Jn 15:12) of love – so, too, in this gospel, there is ultimately only one sin. The Baptist exclaims: Jesus 'takes away the sin of the world!' (Jn 1:29); he does not say: the 'sins' of the world. All sin is rooted in the refusal to accept Jesus, 'the light of the world' (Jn 8:12; 9:5).

The Spirit will show righteousness clearly for what it truly is: that is, who is in the right – Jesus, not the world. Again, Jesus explains why: 'because I am going to the Father,' he says, referring to his victorious return through his passion-resurrection (Jn 16:10; cf 14:31; 16:33). And he adds: 'You will see me no longer' (Jn 16:10) – that is, in his mortal flesh. He will be invisible to the naked eye, but visible to the eyes of faith (cf Jn 14:17).

The Spirit will also bring to light the true meaning of judgement, 'because the ruler of this world,' as Jesus explains, 'has been condemned' (Jn 16:11; cf 12:31). The phrase used here is, literally, 'has been judged (*kekritai*)'. Jesus had already promised, in anticipation of his passion-resurrection: 'Now is the judgement of this world; now the ruler of this world will be driven out' (Jn 12:31). But he had also clarified the meaning of 'judgement': 'And this is the judgement, that the light has come into the world, and people loved darkness rather than light' (Jn 3:19). In John, judgment is self-judgment, or more precisely self-condemnation: a choice for darkness in preference to the light. Jesus says, 'I have come as light into the world, so that everyone who believes in me should not remain in the darkness. I do not judge anyone who hears my words and does not keep them, for I came not to judge the world, but to save the world. The one who rejects me and does not receive my word has a judge; on the last day the word that I have spoken will serve as judge' (Jn 12:46-48). Indeed, Jesus came for division (cf Lk 2:34; 12:51), 'decision' (*krima*, Jn 9:39) on our part – with a challenge freely to accept or to reject the truth of his word. To reject it is to condemn oneself, to embrace willingly the darkness of untruth. To accept it is to be drawn by the Spirit of truth 'out of darkness into his marvellous light' (1 Pet 2:9).

The challenge for everyone who wishes to pray is to make a critical decision to turn away from the darkness of sin and to reach out towards the One who is the splendour of light and truth – Righteousness itself. The Spirit, as a witness to Jesus in the depths of our hearts, is always there to help us.

For Pondering and Prayer

1. John's teaching on the Holy Spirit is contained within the framework of two explicit references to the Spirit (Jn 1:32-33; 20:19-22). How do these references complement each other?

2. The Spirit's way of teaching differs from, and continues, that of Jesus during his ministry. Compare the two, while considering not just the content but also the way of teaching.

3. The Spirit is a witness. In what way does the Spirit as witness in John differ from, and complement, the teaching of the other evangelists on the Spirit's witness (cf Mk 13:9-11; Mt 10:16-20; Lk 12:11-12)?

A GUIDED *LECTIO DIVINA*

The gift of the Spirit (Jn 20:19-22)
When it was evening on that day, the first day of the week, and the doors of the house where the disciples had met were locked for fear of the Jews, Jesus came and stood among them and said: 'Peace be with you.' After he said this, he showed them his hands and his side. Then the disciples rejoiced when they saw the Lord. Jesus said to them again, 'Peace be with you. As the Father has sent me, so I send you.' When he had said this, he breathed on them and said to them, 'Receive the Holy Spirit.'

Reading
Relax. Invoke the Holy Spirit. Then read this passage slowly, attentively and reverently, with mind and heart open to receive the word, ready to respond to whatever it asks of you. Know that it is a word of love from God addressed to you personally. Reread it two or three times – calmly, quietly and without haste.

Meditation
Take a word or phrase that comes to you freely while reading this passage. For example: 'fear'. Recall a time when you experi-

enced fear. Ponder on what might have allayed it. Think of an occasion when the disciples were afraid: for example, when they were storm-tossed on the sea. Jesus said to them: 'Take heart, it is I; do not be afraid' (Mt 14:27). What is this telling you about where to find true peace?

Look at the change in the frightened disciples after Jesus entered the room: 'They rejoiced.' Ponder the gifts he offered his disciples that helped change their lives: peace, joy, the Holy Spirit. Can you recall another occasion in the gospels when someone cried out in joy? For example: 'My Spirit rejoices in God my Saviour' (Lk 1:47). What does this tell you about true joy?

Prayer

Jesus said to his disciples, 'Peace be with you.' Know that he is offering you this same gift of peace. Let your heart go out freely to accept it. Your dialogue with Jesus might run somewhat like this: 'Jesus, I know that I am sometimes frightened because of the times I have wandered from your peace. I thank you for the gift of peace. I come to you now with an open heart as I listen again to your words: "Receive the Holy Spirit." Come into my heart, Spirit of Jesus.'

Contemplation

Stand before the risen Jesus, gazing silently on 'the one whom they have pierced' (Jn 19:37) as he speaks to you now without noise of words. Surrender quietly to the action of the Spirit. He will lead you ever more deeply into the mystery of God, revealed in the passion-resurrection of his Son. Remain docile to the promptings of the Spirit, opening yourself to his transforming touch as he delicately traces on your heart the features of the crucified-risen Jesus.

Action

We can all so easily 'grieve the Holy Spirit of God' (Eph 4:30) and stifle his call. Remember the words you have just listened to: 'As the Father has sent me, so I send you.' Accept this mission in whatever way is right for you. Resolve to witness to the person of the risen Jesus in your life by radiating him to others through the power of his Spirit alive in you.

Praying with Mary

Discovering the mystery of Mary[1]

As the early church grew in its understanding of the mystery of prayer, so too it grew in its awareness of the mystery of Mary. She is inseparable from her Son and has always remained so in the prayer tradition of the church. But the mystery of the Mother of God, like the mystery of prayer itself, developed only gradually in the gospel tradition.[2]

In Mark, the community of believers, under the action of the Spirit, had already come some way to an understanding of the place of Mary in the plan of redemption – as the mother of Jesus (Mk 6:3). But we find little, in this earliest of the gospels, to suggest the church's developed understanding of Mary's deep spiritual relationship with her Son. The situation is different in the later gospels. Both Matthew and Luke were aware that Jesus was conceived virginally in Mary by the Holy Spirit. This is their special contribution to the Christian tradition. It is a new insight which begins to transform the early community's grasp of the mystery of Mary. In Matthew, we find a moderate development of this understanding; in Luke, the development is dramatic. Later still, we have John, in which the presence of Jesus' mother on Calvary constitutes a radical advance on the common tradition of the other gospels. Our final glimpse of Mary in Acts finds her in the midst of the disciples, constant in prayer (cf Acts 1:14). A unique and silent witness at the heart of a praying church, she is our mother; and a sister, too, who stands beside us and who once walked, like us, in faith – on a pilgrim's journey of prayer.

1. For a more extended treatment of Mary in the gospels, see James McCaffrey, *The Carmelite Charism, op. cit.*, chap 5, 'Mary – Woman of Prayer: A Gospel Exploration', pp 103-23.
2. See the references in chap 1, note 4.

The first disciple

There has been a significant new approach to Marian devotion in recent papal documents. John Paul II, for example, speaks of Mary as the first disciple, which marks a renewed approach to the mystery of Mary in relation to her Son: '*in a sense* Mary as Mother became *the first "disciple" of her Son*,' he writes, 'the first to whom he seemed to say: "Follow me".'[3] Here he is recalling the words of his predecessor, Paul VI, who says: 'She was *the first and the most perfect of Christ's disciples*.'[4] For many, this is a new slant on Mary. In fact, it is as old as the gospels: 'A woman in the crowd raised her voice and said to him, "Blessed is the womb that bore you and the breasts that nursed you!" But he said, "Blessed rather are those who hear the word of God and obey it!"' (Lk 11:27-28). Here, Jesus is only taking up again what he had said earlier in Luke's gospel: 'My mother and my brothers are those who hear the word of God and do it' (Lk 8:21). Yes, it is a great thing to be mother of our Saviour in the flesh, but there is something about her even greater still: to be a disciple, a believer. 'Indeed … she did the Father's will,' Augustine says, 'and it is a greater thing for her that she was Christ's disciple than that she was his mother.'[5] Mary is not on a pedestal: she is part of the human race; she is one-of-us, one-with-us – a believer, a disciple. '[In her faith],' writes John Paul II, 'we can therefore rightly find *a kind of "key"* which unlocks for us the innermost reality of Mary'.[6]

Mary – woman of prayer

As 'the first and the most perfect of Christ's disciples', Mary is the model of prayer for every follower of Christ as the evangelists understand the mystery of prayer, each with his own original slant. Like Mark's ideal disciple, Mary has to grope her way in faith towards an ever-clearer vision of the truth. She experi-

---

3. *Redemptoris Mater (Mother of the Redeemer)* 20.
4. *Marialis Cultus (Devotion to the Blessed Virgin Mary)* 35; italics mine.
5. From Sermon 25, in *Divine Office*, vol III, p 409*.
6. *Redemptoris Mater (Mother of the Redeemer)* 19.

ences the absence of God: 'Your father and I have been searching for you in great anxiety' (Lk 2:48). She walks in darkness and does not always understand: 'They did not understand what he said to them' (Lk 2:50). She knows the pain of inner change in a growing relationship with her Son: 'Did you not know that I must be in my Father's house?' (Lk 2:49). All this is part of Mary's faith journey in openness to the action of the Spirit – her prayer experience. Her prayer resembles the movement of the seed in Mark's parable as it edges unseen through the darkness of the earth into the full light of day (Mk 4:26-29).

In her own way, Mary also teaches us to pray like Matthew's ideal disciple. His gospel reminds us, in the words of Jesus, that 'whoever does the will of my Father in heaven is my brother and sister and mother' (Mt 12:50). To commune with God in such an act of surrender to his will is to do so in harmony with Matthew's essential teaching on prayer for every disciple. It is summed up in his third petition of the Our Father, absent in Luke's version of the same prayer: 'Your will be done' (Mt 6:10). At the annunc-iation, Mary's *fiat* was not just her initial act of surrender in re-sponse to God's will. It was an inner disposition of her heart, en-riching every moment of her life. Her whole being was a living prayer. Her final spoken word in the gospels was an act of sur-render to her Son with advice to others that they, like her, should also do the same: 'Do whatever he tells you' (Jn 2:5).

In Luke, Mary is again the perfect disciple of her Son and, like him, a Spirit-filled witness. She proclaims in her *Magnificat* the good news of the Word enfleshed in her womb. But she has first to listen to that message herself in a dialogue of prayer: 'You will conceive in your womb and bear a son' (Lk 1:31). Mary's ceaseless listening gives meaning to her hidden years of quiet prayer in the obscurity of Nazareth as she daily 'treasured' the words of her Son 'and pondered them in her heart' (cf Lk 2:19, 51). Wordless, she stood powerless on Calvary, at one with her powerless Son – an abiding witness for every disciple to the eloquence of listening in silent prayer.

Every true disciple in John is called to pray 'in the name of

Jesus', as he himself intercedes eternally in the heart of his Father and pleads in union with all believers. We see Mary at Cana interceding with her Son; and we also see her at the foot of the cross, where Jesus leaves her to us as our mother – to guide us, protect us and care for us. She is the perfect model for every disciple who wishes to pray in the spirit of the gospels and in union with the whole church. This is how we find Mary herself with the disciples in Acts, 'constantly devoting themselves to prayer' (Acts 1:14) – Mary at the heart of the praying church, ful-filling her Son's great priestly prayer, 'that they may all be one' (Jn 17:21). Mary is not just a woman of prayer. As a perfect disci-ple of Christ, she is *the* gospel woman of prayer.

APPENDIX

Gospel Prayer Texts

1:35   In the morning, while it was still very dark, he got up and went out to a deserted place, and there he prayed.

3:13   He went up the mountain and called to him those whom he wanted …

6:31   Come away to a deserted place all by yourselves and rest a while.

6:46   He went up on the mountain to pray.

7:6-7   He said to them, 'Isaiah prophesied rightly about you hypocrites, as it is written: "This people honours me with their lips, but their hearts are far from me; in vain do they worship me"' (cf Is 29:13).

9:29   This kind can come out only through prayer.

11:17   Is it not written, 'My house shall be called a house of prayer for all the nations?' (cf Is 56:7).

11:22-25   Have faith in God. Truly I tell you, if you say to this mountain, 'Be taken up and thrown into the sea,' and if you do not doubt in your heart, but believe that what you say will come to pass, it will be done for you. So I tell you, whatever you ask for in prayer, believe that you have received it, and it will be yours. Whenever you stand praying, forgive, if you have anything against anyone; so that your Father in heaven may also forgive you your trespasses.

12:38-40   As he taught, he said, 'Beware of the scribes, who like to walk around in long robes, and to be greeted with respect in the marketplaces, and to have the best seats in the synagogues and places of honour at banquets! They devour widows' houses and for the sake of appearance say long prayers. They will receive the greater condemnation.'

13:18   Pray that it may not be in winter.

13:33   Beware, keep alert [and pray].

14:32-42   They went to a place called Gethsemane; and he said to his disciples: 'Sit here while I pray.' … And he said to them, 'I am deeply grieved, even to death; remain here, and keep awake.' And going a little farther, he threw himself on the ground and prayed that, if it were possible, the hour might pass from him. He said, 'Abba, Father, for you all things are possible; remove this cup from me; yet, not what I want, but what you want.' He came and found them sleeping; and he said to Peter, 'Simon, are you asleep? Could you not keep awake one hour? Keep awake and pray that you may not come into the time of trial; the spirit indeed is willing, but the flesh is weak.' And again he went away and prayed, saying the same words … He came a third time and said to them, 'Are you still sleeping and taking your rest? Enough! … See, my betrayer is at hand.'

15:33-34   When it was noon, darkness came over the whole land until three in the afternoon. At three o'clock Jesus cried out with a loud voice, 'Eloi, Eloi, lema sabachthani?' which means, 'My God, my God, why have you forsaken me?'

PRAYER REFERENCES IN MATTHEW

2:2, 8 ,11   'We [Magi] observed his star at its rising, and have come to pay him homage.' ... 'bring me word so that I [Herod] may also go and pay him homage.' ... [The Magi] knelt down and paid him homage.

5:44   But I say to you, Love your enemies and pray for those who persecute you ...

6:5-15   And whenever you pray, do not be like the hypocrites; for they love to stand and pray in the synagogues and at the street corners, so that they may be seen by others. Truly I tell you, they have received their reward. But whenever you pray, go into your room and shut the door and pray to your Father who is in secret; and your Father who sees in secret will reward you. When you are praying, do not heap up empty phrases as the Gentiles do; for they think that they will be heard because of their many words. Do not be like them, for your Father knows what you need before you ask him. Pray then in this way: Our Father in heaven, hallowed be your name. Your kingdom come. Your will be done, on earth as it is in heaven. Give us this day our daily bread. And forgive us our debts, as we also have forgiven our debtors. And do not bring us to the time of trial, but rescue us from the evil one. For if you forgive others their trespasses, your heavenly Father will also forgive you; but if you do not forgive others, neither will your Father forgive your trespasses.

7:7, 11   Ask, and it will be given you; search, and you will find; knock, and the door will be opened for you ... If you then, who are evil, know how to give good gifts to your children, how much more will your Father in heaven give good things to those who ask him!

9:37-38   Then he said to his disciples, 'The harvest is plenti-
            ful, but the labourers are few; therefore ask the
            Lord of the harvest to send out labourers into his
            harvest.'

11:25-27   At that time Jesus said, 'I thank you, Father, Lord of
            heaven and earth, because you have hidden these
            things from the wise and the intelligent and have
            revealed them to infants; yes, Father, for such was
            your gracious will. All things have been handed
            over to me by my Father; and no one knows the Son
            except the Father, and no one knows the Father ex-
            cept the Son and anyone to whom the Son chooses
            to reveal him.

14:13   Now when Jesus heard this, he withdrew from
            there in a boat to a deserted place by himself.

14:23   And after he had dismissed the crowds, he went up
            the mountain by himself to pray. When evening
            came, he was there alone.

14:33   And those in the boat worshipped him, saying,
            'Truly you are the Son of God.'

15:7-9   You hypocrites! Isaiah prophesied rightly about
            you when he said: 'This people honours me with
            their lips, but their hearts are far from me; in vain
            do they worship me, teaching human precepts as
            doctrines' (cf Is 29:13).

18:19-20   Again, truly I tell you, if two of you agree on earth
            about anything you ask, it will be done for you by
            my Father in heaven. For where two or three are
            gathered in my name, I am there among them.

19:13   Then little children were being brought to him in
            order that he might lay his hands on them and
            pray.

21:13   He said to them, 'It is written, "My house shall be called a house of prayer"; but you are making it a den of robbers' (cf Is 56:7; Jer 7:11).

21:21-22   Jesus answered them, 'Truly I tell you, if you have faith and do not doubt, not only will you do what has been done to the fig tree, but even if you say to this mountain, "Be lifted up and thrown into the sea," it will be done. Whatever you ask for in prayer with faith, you will receive.'

24:4   Beware that no one leads you astray …

24:20   Pray that your flight may not be in winter or on a sabbath.

24:42   Keep awake therefore, for you do not know on what day your Lord is coming.

25:13   Keep awake therefore, for you know neither the day nor the hour.

26:36-46   Then Jesus went with them to a place called Gethsemane; and he said to his disciples, 'Sit here while I go over there and pray.' … Then he said to them, 'I am deeply grieved, even to death; remain here, and stay awake with me.' And going a little farther, he threw himself on the ground and prayed, 'My Father, if it is possible, let this cup pass from me; yet not what I want but what you want.' Then he came to the disciples and found them sleeping; and he said to Peter, 'So, could you not stay awake with me one hour? Stay awake and pray that you may not come into the time of trial; the spirit indeed is willing, but the flesh is weak.' Again he went away for the second time and prayed, 'My Father, if this cannot pass unless I drink it, your will be done.' Again he came and found them sleeping … So leaving them again, he went away and prayed for the third time, saying the same words. Then he came to the disciples and said to them, 'Are you still sleeping and taking your rest? See, the hour is at hand … my betrayer is at hand.'

27:45-46   From noon on, darkness came over the whole land until three in the afternoon. And about three o'clock Jesus cried with a loud voice, 'Eli, Eli, lema sabachthani?' that is, 'My God, my God, why have you forsaken me?'

28:8-9   So they left the tomb quickly with fear and great joy, and ran to tell his disciples. Suddenly Jesus met them and said, 'Greetings!' And they came to him, took hold of his feet, and worshipped him.

28:16-17   Now the eleven disciples went to Galilee, to the mountain to which Jesus had directed them. When they saw him, they worshipped him …

PRAYER REFERENCES IN LUKE

1:10   Now at the time of the incense offering, the whole assembly of the people was praying outside.

1:13   But the angel said to him, 'Do not be afraid, Zechariah, for your prayer has been heard. Your wife Elizabeth will bear you a son …'

1:38   Then Mary said, 'Here am I, the servant of the Lord; let it be with me according to your word.'

1:46   And Mary said, 'My soul magnifies the Lord …'

2:19-20   But Mary treasured all these words and pondered them in her heart. The shepherds returned, glorifying and praising God for all they had heard and seen, as it had been told them.

2:28-30   Simeon took [the child Jesus] in his arms and praised God, saying, 'Master, now you are dismissing your servant in peace, according to your word; for my eyes have seen your salvation …'

2:37-38   [Anna] never left the temple but worshipped there with fasting and prayer night and day. At that moment she came, and began to praise God and to speak about the child [Jesus] …

3:21   Now when all the people were baptised, and when Jesus also had been baptised and was praying, the heaven was opened.

4:42   At daybreak he departed and went into a deserted place. And the crowds were looking for him; and when they reached him, they wanted to prevent him from leaving them.

5:15-16   But now more than ever the word about Jesus spread abroad; many crowds would gather to hear him and to be cured of their diseases. But he would withdraw to deserted places and pray.

5:33   Then they said to him, 'John's disciples, like the disciples of the Pharisees, frequently fast and pray, but your disciples eat and drink.'

6:12-13   Now during those days he went out to the mountain to pray; and he spent the night in prayer to God. And when day came, he called his disciples and chose twelve of them, whom he also named apostles.

6:27-28   But I say to you that listen, Love your enemies, do good to those who hate you, bless those who curse you, pray for those who abuse you.

9:18   Once when Jesus was praying alone, with only the disciples near him, he asked them, 'Who do the crowds say that I am?'

9:28-29   Now about eight days after these sayings Jesus took with him Peter and John and James, and went up on the mountain to pray. And while he was praying, the appearance of his face changed, and his clothes became dazzling white.

10:2   He said to them, 'The harvest is plentiful, but the labourers are few; therefore ask the Lord of the harvest to send out labourers into his harvest.'

10:21-22   At that same hour Jesus rejoiced in the Holy Spirit and said, 'I thank you, Father, Lord of heaven and earth, because you have hidden these things from the wise and the intelligent and have revealed them to infants; yes, Father, for such was your gracious will. All things have been handed over to me by my Father; and no one knows who the Son is except the Father, or who the Father is except the Son and anyone to whom the Son chooses to reveal him.'

10:38-42   Now as they went on their way, he entered a certain village, where a woman named Martha welcomed him into her home. She had a sister named Mary, who sat at the Lord's feet and listened to what he was saying. But Martha was distracted by her many tasks; so she came to him and asked, 'Lord, do you not care that my sister has left me to do all the work by myself? Tell her then to help me.' But the Lord answered her, 'Martha, Martha, you are worried and distracted by many things; there is need of only one thing. Mary has chosen the better part, which will not be taken away from her.'

11:1-13   He was praying in a certain place, and after he had finished, one of his disciples said to him, 'Lord, teach us to pray, as John taught his disciples.' He said to them, 'When you pray, say: Father, hallowed be your name. Your kingdom come. Give us each day our daily bread. And forgive us our sins, for we ourselves forgive everyone indebted to us.

And do not bring us to the time of trial.' And he said to them, 'Suppose one of you has a friend, and you go to him at midnight and say to him, "Friend, lend me three loaves of bread; for a friend of mine has arrived" ... because of his persistence he will get up and give him whatever he needs. So I say to you, Ask, and it will be given you; search, and you will find; knock, and the door will be opened for you. For everyone who asks receives, and everyone who searches finds, and for everyone who knocks, the door will be opened ... If you then, who are evil, know how to give good gifts to your children, how much more will the heavenly Father give the Holy Spirit to those who ask him!'

18:1-3, 7-8   Then Jesus told them a parable about their need to pray always and not to lose heart. He said, 'In a certain city there was a judge who neither feared God nor had respect for people. In that city there was a widow who kept coming to him and saying, "Grant me justice against my opponent." ... And will not God grant justice to his chosen ones who cry to him day and night? Will he delay long in helping them? I tell you, he will quickly grant justice to them.'

18:9-10, 13   He also told this parable to some who trusted in themselves that they were righteous and regarded others with contempt: 'Two men went up to the temple to pray, one a Pharisee and the other a tax collector ... the tax collector, standing far off, would not even look up to heaven, but was beating his breast and saying, "God, be merciful to me, a sinner!"'

19:45-46   Then he entered the temple and began to drive out those who were selling things there; and he said, 'It is written, "My house shall be a house of prayer"' (cf Is 56:7).

20:46-47   Beware of the scribes, who like to walk around in long robes, and love to be greeted with respect in the marketplaces, and to have the best seats in the synagogues and places of honour at banquets. They devour widows' houses and for the sake of appearance say long prayers. They will receive the greater condemnation.

21:36   Be alert at all times, praying that you may have the strength to escape all these things that will take place, and to stand before the Son of Man.

22:31-32   Simon, Simon, listen! Satan has demanded to sift all of you like wheat, but I have prayed for you that your own faith may not fail; and you, when once you have turned back, strengthen your brothers.

22:39-46   He came out and went, as was his custom, to the Mount of Olives; and the disciples followed him. When he reached the place, he said to them, 'Pray that you may not come into the time of trial.' Then he withdrew from them about a stone's throw, knelt down, and prayed, 'Father, if you are willing, remove this cup from me; yet, not my will but yours be done.' Then an angel from heaven appeared to him and gave him strength. In his anguish he prayed more earnestly, and his sweat became like great drops of blood falling down on the ground. When he got up from prayer, he came to the disciples and found them sleeping because of grief, and he said to them, 'Why are you sleeping? Get up and pray that you may not come into the time of trial.'

23:34   Then Jesus said, 'Father, forgive them; for they do not know what they are doing.'

23:46-47   Then Jesus, crying with a loud voice, said, 'Father, into your hands I commend my spirit.' Having said this, he breathed his last. When the centurion saw what had taken place, he praised God and said, 'Certainly this man was innocent.'

24:5   The women were terrified and bowed their faces to the ground, but the men said to them: 'Why do you look for the living among the dead? He is not here, but has risen.'

24:50-53   Then he led them out as far as Bethany, and, lifting up his hands, he blessed them. While he was blessing them, he withdrew from them and was carried up into heaven. And they worshipped him, and returned to Jerusalem with great joy; and they were continually in the temple blessing God.

PRAYER REFERENCES IN JOHN

4:21-24   Woman, believe me, the hour is coming when you will worship the Father neither on this mountain nor in Jerusalem. You worship what you do not know; we worship what we know, for salvation is from the Jews. But the hour is coming, and is now here, when the true worshippers will worship the Father in spirit and truth, for the Father seeks such as these to worship him. God is spirit, and those who worship him must worship in spirit and truth.

6:15   When Jesus realised that they were about to come and take him by force to make him king, he withdrew again to the mountain by himself.

11:41-42   Jesus looked upward and said, 'Father, I thank you for having heard me. I knew that you always hear me, but I have said this for the sake of the crowd standing here, so that they may believe that you sent me.'

12:27-28   Now my soul is troubled. And what should I say – 'Father, save me from this hour?' … Father, glorify your name.

14:13-14   I will do whatever you ask in my name, so that the Father may be glorified in the Son. If in my name you ask me for anything, I will do it.

16:23-27   Very truly, I tell you, if you ask anything of the Father in my name, he will give it to you. Until now you have not asked for anything in my name. Ask and you will receive, so that your joy may be complete. I have said these things to you in figures of speech. The hour is coming when I will no longer speak to you in figures, but will tell you plainly of the Father. On that day you will ask in my name. I do not say to you that I will ask the Father on your behalf; for the Father himself loves you, because you have loved me and have believed that I came from God (cf Jn 15:16).

19:37   'They will look on the one whom they have pierced' (cf Zech 12:10).

PRIESTLY PRAYER

(John 17)

1   After Jesus had spoken these words, he looked up to heaven and said, 'Father, the hour has come; glorify your Son so that the Son may glorify you,

2   since you have given him authority over all people, to give eternal life to all whom you have given him.

3   And this is eternal life, that they may know you, the only true God, and Jesus Christ whom you have sent.

4   I glorified you on earth by finishing the work that you gave me to do.

5   So now, Father, glorify me in your own presence with the glory that I had in your presence before the world existed.

6   I have made your name known to those whom you gave me from the world. They were yours, and you gave them to me, and they have kept your word.

7   Now they know that everything you have given me is from you;

8   for the words that you gave to me I have given to them, and they have received them and know in truth that I came from you; and they have believed that you sent me.

9   I am asking on their behalf; I am not asking on behalf of the world, but on behalf of those whom you gave me, because they are yours.

10   All mine are yours, and yours are mine; and I have been glorified in them.

11   And now I am no longer in the world, but they are in the world, and I am coming to you. Holy Father, protect them in your name that you have given me, so that they may be one, as we are one.

12   While I was with them, I protected them in your name that you have given me. I guarded them, and not one of them was lost except the one destined to be lost, so that the scripture might be fulfilled.

13   But now I am coming to you, and I speak these things in the world so that they may have my joy made complete in themselves.

14   I have given them your word, and the world has hated them because they do not belong to the world, just as I do not belong to the world.

15   I am not asking you to take them out of the world, but I ask you to protect them from the evil one.

16   They do not belong to the world, just as I do not belong to the world.

17   Sanctify them in the truth; your word is truth.

18   As you have sent me into the world, so I have sent them into the world.

19   And for their sakes I sanctify myself, so that they also may be sanctified in truth.

20   I ask not only on behalf of these, but also on behalf of those who will believe in me through their word,

21   that they may all be one. As you, Father, are in me and I am in you, may they also be in us, so that the world may believe that you have sent me.

22   The glory that you have given me I have given them, so that they may be one, as we are one,

23   I in them and you in me, that they may become completely one, so that the world may know that you have sent me and have loved them even as you have loved me.

24   Father, I desire that those also, whom you have given me, may be with me where I am, to see my glory, which you have given me because you loved me before the foundation of the world.

25   Righteous Father, the world does not know you, but I know you; and these know that you have sent me.

26   I made your name known to them, and I will make it known, so that the love with which you have loved me may be in them, and I in them.

PRAYER REFERENCES TO THE SPIRIT
(John)

1:32-34   And John testified, 'I saw the Spirit descending
           from heaven like a dove, and it remained on him. I
           myself did not know him, but the one who sent me
           to baptise with water said to me, "He on whom you
           see the Spirit descend and remain is the one who
           baptises with the Holy Spirit." And I myself have
           seen and have testified that this is the Son of God.'

3:3-8   Jesus answered him, 'Very truly, I tell you, no one
           can see the kingdom of God without being born
           from above.' Nicodemus said to him, 'How can
           anyone be born after having grown old? Can one
           enter a second time into the mother's womb and be
           born?' Jesus answered, 'Very truly, I tell you, no
           one can enter the kingdom of God without being
           born of water and Spirit. What is born of the flesh is
           flesh, and what is born of the Spirit is spirit. Do not
           be astonished that I said to you, "You must be born
           from above." The wind blows where it chooses,
           and you hear the sound of it, but you do not know
           where it comes from or where it goes. So it is with
           everyone who is born of the Spirit.'

3:34-35   He whom God has sent speaks the words of God,
           for he gives the Spirit without measure. The Father
           loves the Son and has placed all things in his hands.

4:21-24   Jesus said to her, 'Woman, believe me, the hour is
           coming when you will worship the Father neither
           on this mountain nor in Jerusalem. You worship
           what you do not know; we worship what we know,
           for salvation is from the Jews. But the hour is com-
           ing, and is now here, when the true worshippers
           will worship the Father in spirit and truth, for the
           Father seeks such as these to worship him. God is

spirit, and those who worship him must worship in spirit and truth.'

6:63   It is the spirit that gives life; the flesh is useless. The words that I have spoken to you are spirit and life.

7:39   Now he said this about the Spirit, which believers in him were to receive; for as yet there was no Spirit, because Jesus was not yet glorified.

19:30   When Jesus had received the wine, he said, 'It is finished.' Then he bowed his head and gave up his spirit.

20:22   When he had said this, he breathed on them and said to them, 'Receive the Holy Spirit.'

PARACLETE PASSAGES
(John)

Teacher

14:16-17   And I will ask the Father, and he will give you another Advocate, to be with you forever. This is the Spirit of truth, whom the world cannot receive, because it neither sees him nor knows him. You know him, because he abides with you, and he will be in you.

14:25-26   I have said these things to you while I am still with you. But the Advocate, the Holy Spirit, whom the Father will send in my name, will teach you everything, and remind you of all that I have said to you.

16:12-15   I still have many things to say to you, but you cannot bear them now. When the Spirit of truth comes, he will guide you into all the truth; for he will not speak on his own, but will speak whatever he hears, and he will declare to you the things that are to come. He will glorify me, because he will take what is mine and declare it to you. All that the

Father has is mine. For this reason I said that he will take what is mine and declare it to you.

Witness

15:26-27   When the Advocate comes, whom I will send to you from the Father, the Spirit of truth who comes from the Father, he will testify on my behalf. You also are to testify because you have been with me from the beginning.

16:7-11   Nevertheless I tell you the truth: it is to your advantage that I go away, for if I do not go away, the Advocate will not come to you; but if I go, I will send him to you. And when he comes, he will prove the world wrong about sin and righteousness and judgement: about sin, because they do not believe in me; about righteousness, because I am going to the Father and you will see me no longer; about judgement, because the ruler of this world has been condemned.